COMMUNICATION STRATEGIES 4

Jun Liu

Kathryn Harper

CENGAGE
Learning™

Australia • Brazil • Japan • Korea • Mexico • Singapore • Spain • United Kingdom • United States

Communication Strategies 4
Jun Liu and Kathryn Harper

Publishing Director: Paul Tan
Editorial Manager: Andrew Robinson
Editor: Andrew Jessop

Senior Product Manager: Michael Cahill
Interior Design: Pixel Production Works
Printer: Seng Lee Press

The publisher would like to thank The Kobal Collection for their permission to reproduce photographs on the following pages:

6: The Whole Ten Yards MHF Zweite Film Academy / The Kobal Collection / Frank Masi; 12: The Beach 20th Century Fox / The Kobal Collection / Peter Mountain; 18: 15 Minutes Industry Ent/New Line / The Kobal Collection / Philip Caruso; 24: The Nutty Professor Universal / The Kobal Collection / Bruce MC Broom; 30: Live Free Or Die Hard 20th Century Fox / The Kobal Collection / Frank Masi; 36: The Pursuit Of Happyness Columbia / The Kobal Collection / Zade Rosenthal; 42: Medicine Man Cinergi / The Kobal Collection; 48: Snakes On A Plane New Line / The Kobal Collection / James Dittiger; 54: Marie Antoinette Colombia/Pathe/Sony / The Kobal Collection / Leigh Johnson; 60: Maid In Manhattan Columbia / The Kobal Collection / Barry Wetcher; 66: The Fan Tri-Star/Mandalay / The Kobal Collection; 72: The Day After Tomorrow 20th Century Fox / The Kobal Collection; 78: 13 Going On 30 Colombia Tri Star / The Kobal Collection / Sue Melinda Gordon; 984: Mean Girls Paramount / The Kobal Collection / Michael Gibson; 90: Boiler Room New Line / The Kobal Collection / David Lee

The publisher would like to thank the following for their permission to reproduce photographs on the following pages:

© 2007 Jupiterimages Corporation: 08, 14, 15, 16, 17, 19, 21, 23, 25, 27, 28, 31, 33, 34, 35, 37, 38, 39, 40, 44, 45, 46, 49, 50, 51, 57, 59, 61, 63, 65, 68, 69, 70, 71, 75 (top), 76, 77, 81, 82, 83, 86, 87, 88, 89, 92, 93, 98.

© 2007 Getty Images Sales Singapore Pte Ltd: 09, 20, 25, 26, 29, 32, 56, 62, 71, 74, 75 (bottom), 80, 96, 97

Please note, that all people shown are models and are used only for illustrative purposes.

For permission to use material from this text or product, email to **asia.publishing@cengage.com**

ISBN-13: 978-981-4232-67-8
ISBN-10: 981-4232-67-X

Cengage Learning Asia Pte Ltd
5 Shenton Way #01-01
UIC Building
Singapore 068808
Tel: (65) 6410 1200
Fax: (65) 6410 1208

Cengage Learning products are represented in Canada by Nelson Education, Ltd.

For product information, visit **www.cengageasia.com**

Printed in Singapore
2 3 4 5 6 – 14 13 12 11 10

FOREWORD

Learners are often able to strike up a conversation in English, but after a few minutes, they soon get tongue-tied when the conversation moves beyond the surface level. I firmly believe that to overcome this, students should concentrate on reaching a reasonably high level of communicative competence as quickly as possible. Once this is attained, learners will have elevated themselves from language learners to language users and will then be in a better position to build on this knowledge. They will also be better prepared to deal with the range of exams that many of them now face, including CET 4, IELTS, or TOEFL.

Only by getting into the substance of communication can we move beyond formulaic English and become language users. This textbook series is designed to enable you to be excellent strategic language users. It is my hope that you will enjoy using the book to further your communication strategies and become excellent users of English in real communication.

Jun Liu
Professor and Head of English Department
University of Arizona

ACKNOWLEDGMENTS

I would like to thank Kathryn Harper, my co-author of this book, for her great collaboration and enthusiastic work. I am indebted to everyone at Cengage Learning, in particular, Paul Tan, Andrew Robinson, Andrew Jessop, and Hoi Kin Chiu, for their trust, encouragement, and great assistance in the process of the book production.

I would also like to thank the professionals who have offered invaluable comments and suggestions during the development of the course, in particular:

Chen Lijiang – *Associate Professor, Shanghai International Studies University*
Fan Xiangtao – *Associate Professor, Nanjing University of Aeronautics and Astronautics*
Gao Dexin – *Associate Professor , Shandong Liyi Normal University*
Jia Zhongheng – *Associate Professor, Tong Ji University*
Li Zhiling – *Professor, Shandong Agricultural University*
Quan Jianqiang – *Vice-Dean of English Department, East China Normal University*
Tao Qing – *Professor, Shanghai Jiao Tong University*
Wan Hua – *Dean of English Department, Shanghai University*
Wei Xiangqing – *Professor, Nanjing University*
Zhang Yi – *Dean of English Department, East China Normal University*
Zong Ruikun – *Professor, Shanghai Xing Jian College*

Jun Liu

TABLE OF CONTENTS

DISCUSSION STRATEGIES		SPEECHES
Using language of mediation	Is there any way we can work this out? I can live with that as long as… It would be helpful if…	Advice to neighbors
Asking critical questions	How can you say…? I think you're mistaken… What makes you so sure…?	A new development model that works
Asking for clarification	Do you mean that…? Do you believe that…? You're implying that…	A book festival
Taking exception (casual)	I'm not saying … but… Are you kidding/serious? I can't believe you think that…	Being positive about your body
Supporting statements	For example,… Look at… Did you know/realize that…?	A presentation on Internet safety
Prompting for more information	Is that right/so? You must have been/felt… That couldn't have been…	My ideal relationship
Agreeing	I can see/understand that. I know/see what you mean. You have a good point.	A presentation on health treatments
Convincing and suggesting	Look at the facts… It will be easier if… All you have to do is…	It's safe to fly
Avoiding questions	I'll give that some thought… I can't answer that, but… There are more important things…	A radio commercial
Complaining	That's not really the issue… You can't expect… I have the right…	Know your consumer rights
Acknowledging emotions	I really sympathize/feel for you. That must have been… I do understand…	Keep cool
Expressing concern	I plan to act more carefully when… I can't help thinking that… It makes me uneasy that…	A debate about the environment
An alternative point of view	…doesn't have to be like that. It can… You could think of it another way… On the other hand…	What's best for an elderly relative
Constructive criticism	Maybe you could… You don't have to be… If you … that won't get you very far.	Reporting an incident
Ending a conversation	Why don't we… Can we just agree to disagree? I'm really tired of talking about…	Present yourself

Neighbors

Four years ago, Zack Bower (38) and his wife Linda (36) moved from their small, city apartment to a house in a pretty village surrounded by beautiful countryside. However, they recently moved back to their old third-floor apartment. They keep the windows closed because of the noise and the pollution and they miss the rural views, but they are now much happier.

Their idyllic ideas of rural life didn't match the realities. Linda explains, "We moved to the countryside because we thought that the quality of life would be so much better. But we found that it just didn't suit us. We were seen as newcomers and no one in the village would talk to us even though they were watching everything we did. It was really uncomfortable."

The couple made an effort to get to know their neighbors, but continued to find life hard. "We just didn't see eye to eye on anything. They were suspicious, small minded, and not very sophisticated." Zack says,

adding, "Basically we could never really be ourselves. They criticized everything we did. We really felt that they were invading our space and our privacy."

The tensions started to escalate and things got pretty hostile for a while. The few friends they had were other families that, like them, had recently moved to the village.

It was harder for their two teenage children. "Being new and the only mixed-race kids for miles around, our children were constantly picked on at school. Basically, our rural idyll became a rural prison." Linda says.

Much as they liked being surrounded by beautiful countryside, they found they were city folk at heart and they never learned to cope with things such as roosters crowing first thing every morning and the country smells. There was little for them to do and they ended up going back to the city most weekends. Plus, living in an

isolated village with no bus service meant they had to drive everywhere, becoming a taxi service for their children especially in the school vacations.

They don't regret their years in the countryside. Zack explains, "We were restless and needed a change. We thought life would be better in a smaller community where everybody knew everyone else. But we found that's just not for us. Here in the city, we don't really know our neighbors, but we don't care. We feel accepted without having to really interact with anyone. Everyone sort of follows a set of unwritten rules – our neighbors never bother us and we don't bother them. If there's any noise we just bang on the door and it's over. Nothing hostile, no hard feelings – just get on with life. If we need anything, we know they are there and will help us. It doesn't mean we're unsociable, but we choose who we see and when we see them."

VOCABULARY

Here are some words that will be useful in this unit. How many do you know? Work with a partner to figure out the meaning of any words that you don't know.

amicable	escalate	invade	rude
compromise	hostile	mediate	suspicious
confront	inconsiderate	misunderstanding	tension
distant	intervene	personality clash	threaten

What other words and phrases do you know related to the topic?

VOCABULARY ACTIVITIES

A. Read each definition. Fill in the blank with words from the list above.

1. An agreement in which each side settles for less than they would like. _____
2. To face someone with something that bothers you. _____
3. To come between two parties, often in a helpful way. _____
4. To try and settle a disagreement. _____
5. When two people are very different. _____

B. Fill in the blanks with words from the list above to complete the text. Use the correct word form.

Most people will experience a problem with a neighbor at some time in their lives. This can range from mild 1. _____ to extreme cases where there is 2. _____ behavior. Most people want 3. _____ relations with their neighbors but will settle for 4. _____ but polite relationships. However for some reason, whether it's a 5. _____ or the fact the some people are just 6. _____ or downright 7. _____ , a lot of neighbor relations do breakdown. Sometimes it just starts with a slight 8. _____ but then it escalates. It's best to 9. _____ the neighbor directly when there's a problem, but that's not always easy if the person is 10. _____ . Sometimes you need to turn to someone to 11. _____ or even call on the authorities to 12. _____ in serious cases. Why is it so difficult to live together? Are there just too many people, making us feel that our space is being 13. _____ ?

Work with a partner. Read the paragraph aloud and compare your answers.

Why do you think some people have trouble getting along with their neighbors?

GRAPHIC ORGANIZER

Look at these problem areas and give examples for each. Work with a partner. Compare your ideas.

NOISE	SMELLS	MESS	APPEARANCE	BEHAVIOR

POINTS OF VIEW *Neighbors need to find a compromise.*

PRE-LISTENING QUESTIONS

1. Have you ever had to confront a neighbor about a problem? Was it difficult?
2. What's the best approach to take when you have a problem with a neighbor?

SITUATION: *Nina is talking to her neighbor about a problem.*

Nina	Hi Sandra. Do you have a minute to talk?
Sandra	Sure. What can I do for you?
Nina	Well, it's your new dog. He's constantly barking when you're out. What's worse is that he causes all the other dogs in the neighborhood to bark, too.
Sandra	I'm sorry about that.
Nina	Well, it's very annoying. I'm trying to study for some very important exams and I can't concentrate. It's really stressing me out.
Sandra	I do apologize. I had no idea. I'm away so much.
Nina	I know. That's why I'm telling you now. But it's also why he's barking so much. He's lonely. You shouldn't keep a dog like that locked in a house alone all day.
Sandra	I know. But there have been so many robberies recently and I thought having a dog would help. Plus he makes me feel safer when I'm on my own at home, especially at night. I just don't feel comfortable going out by myself anymore.
Nina	Well, I can understand that. Crime is getting pretty bad. It's gotten worse since they turned Mrs. Thomson's house into a shelter for the homeless.
Sandra	I don't think there's a link. But no one can deny there have been more problems since the shelter opened.
Nina	Look, I can understand why you want a dog. Is there any way we can work this out?
Sandra	Well, the big problem seems to be that he misses me. Perhaps I could try to come home during my lunch break, if that would help.
Nina	I think it might. Thanks. It's only the barking that's a problem. I could take him for a short walk a couple of times a day if you like.
Sandra	Oh, that would be great. You wouldn't mind?
Nina	I'll do it if it helps keep him quiet. The real problem seems to be the rising crime rate though. Perhaps we should talk to the other people in the street and set up a neighborhood watch or something. What do you think?
Sandra	Sounds like a good idea. Let's involve the shelter though. I don't want them to think that they're not welcome here.
Nina	Okay. I'll look into it.

CHECK FOR UNDERSTANDING

1. Why does Sandra's dog bark so much?
2. What solution does Sandra come up with? Why is that a compromise?
3. What does Nina offer to do to help pacify the dog?
4. What else does Nina agree to do? Why?
5. Think of other suggestions for resolving the problems.

Work with a partner. Compare your answers.

Quick Fact
In 2006, a Japanese woman who repeatedly screamed insults and played loud music while beating a mattress on her balcony was sent to prison for one year.

PRACTICE AND DISCUSSION

PERSONALIZATION

Complete these sentences with your own ideas.

Dogs and other animals can be...

If something disturbs me when I'm trying to study, I...

People with noisy animals should...

It's important to inform your neighbors about what you're doing because...

When dealing with problem neighbors, it's a good idea to...

Now share your sentences with a classmate.

DISCUSSION STRATEGIES - Using language of mediation

In a difficult discussion, it's important to remain as calm and reasonable as possible. Listed below are some expressions we can use to mediate.

Is there any way we can work this out?
I can live/cope with that as long as...
Just keep me informed...
I could ... if that would help.
there are a number of solutions...

Is there anything you can do about it?
It would be very helpful if...
What about...
...is actually causing problems for me
Could we try...

Think of more examples.

Discussion Strategy in Action

Listen to the conversations. Is the mediator effective? Write the expressions that indicate this.

Was the mediation successful?		Why/Why not?
1.	Yes ☐ No ☐	_____
2.	Yes ☐ No ☐	_____
3.	Yes ☐ No ☐	_____

Discussion Practice

Work with a partner. How would you respond if you were the mediator in these situations?

1. I can't help it if my children are noisy. They're little and they have to play. There's no park nearby.
2. I don't think that I play my music too loudly.
3. I have to have a security system. My insurance company requires it. I can't help it if the security lights keep coming on every time people walk past the house.
4. Just because we share a kitchen doesn't mean he can take my food whenever he feels like it. He should buy his own!

FURTHER ACTIVITIES

ROLE PLAY

> **Brainstorming:**
> Think of things that can be very annoying to people living in small apartments with thin walls.

Work with a partner. For each of these situations, try to find a solution to resolve the problem:

1. A: You are a student in the final year of medical school. You have to study and you are very unhappy about the noise from B's room.

    B: You are a musician who is preparing to record your first rock album next month and must practice.

2. A: You let your bath overflow. The ceiling in the apartment below was damaged. You don't have the money to pay for the repairs or insurance.

    B: You live in the flat below. You like everything to be perfect and want the damaged ceiling to be repaired immediately.

3. A: New neighbors move in. They look different, speak loudly, and play strange music. You don't like the way their food smells.

    B: You have just moved into the apartment with your family. You don't know the local customs. One neighbor seems unfriendly, won't talk to you, or help you.

ACTIVITY

How well do you get on with your neighbors?

Complete the questionnaire on pages 96 and 97. Work with a partner. Discuss your answers. Consider the vocabulary used in each question. Provide additional examples of vocabulary that might have been used instead.

Discuss your answers and additional vocabulary with the class.

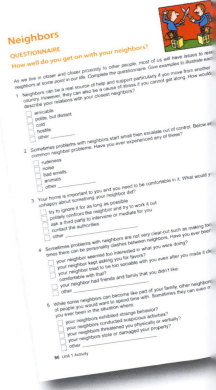

SPEECHES - Advice to neighbors

Imagine that you are a psychologist going on the radio to give general advice on being a good neighbor and provide help for people who may have problems with their neighbors.

Consider the following:

- What they want to achieve when they talk to their neighbors.
- The most effective way of talking to problem neighbors.
- How firm they need to be.
- Ideas for preparing themselves to talk to problem neighbors.
- Strategies for getting what you want.

Give your talk to the class or a group of students as if it is going out on the radio.

Ask for questions.

CONSOLIDATION AND RECYCLING

BUILDING VOCABULARY

Look at the prefixes and suffixes below and decide which ones go at the beginning and which ones go at the end of word fragments. Add them to correctly complete the sentences. Caution! Some take both a suffix and a prefix and may require a change in spelling.

com	able	ness	con	ate	tion	ing
ality	mis	ed	in	inter	stand	un

1. I wanted my neighbors stop putting their garbage near my door, but when I spoke to them about it, they were really _____(compromise).
2. I try to have amicable relationships with the people next door but they are often extremely _____(consider).
3. _____ (rude) and bad manners are two things I just can't tolerate.
4. That man has a terribly aggressive _____(person). I'm surprised he gets along with anyone at all.
5. Don't _____(understand) me. I want to get along with my neighbor, but I can't accept their screaming and fighting at all hours of the night.
6. My neighbors are so loud that I feel as if my home is being _____(vade) by their noise.
7. Their fighting got so bad that in the end, police _____(intervene) was necessary.
8. Normally, my neighbor is the most _____(threaten) person you can meet. But when he's had a few drinks, he turns into a monster.

Work with your partner and think of other words that can take these prefixes and suffixes.

WRITING

Imagine that you have had problems with neighbors. You now want to lodge an official complaint with the company that manages your building.

Consider the following:

- What exactly has happened.
- How it has affected you.
- How it is an infringement of your rights.
- What you want the company to do for you.

This would be a formal letter. You need to be accurate.

Quick Fact
Neighbor noise is considered a problem to some extent by around 30% of people in England, and a serious problem by 8%.

REFLECTION

1. How important is it to get along with your neighbors for peace of mind?
2. What is the best way to resolve a difficult problem with neighbors?
3. Would you consider moving if relations with neighbors became too difficult?

Tourism

Shangri-La or Paradise Lost? – It is wonderful to travel and discover new cultures and landscapes, but do you ever think about the effects tourism can have on the places you visit?

Countries with fragile economies and infrastructure may see tourism as a great opportunity for economic and social development. However, tourism developments may not always be the answer to a country's economic woes and they can sometimes do more harm than good.

Every year, around 140 million people travel from an industrialized country to a developing one. Many will be on a holiday that will have cost thousands of dollars. The money spent by holidaymakers is an important source of income to the people living in the destination countries. However, often less than half the revenue from the trip actually stays in that country – sometimes the 'revenue leakage' can be as much as 80 percent.

In addition, moderate or mass tourism can put a huge strain on the developing country's society and its infrastructure such as roads, water, electricity, and sewage treatment. That's not to mention the environmental impact.

Take for example, Jamaica. This Caribbean island paradise has been a mass tourist destination for many years and its economy is partly dependent on tourism. Yet tourism has put a huge strain on the natural resources of the country and is, in part, responsible for pollution, loss of animal and plant species, coral reef destruction, deforestation, and erosion of beaches.

The local community suffers from loss of natural public beaches, water shortages, and a significant amount of the food used by the hotels is imported rather than being purchased from local farms. A lot of the hotels are gated from the rest of the community because of high crime rates, but in some ways this further isolates the tourists from the local population – other than those employed as staff at the resorts.

Bhutan's approach to tourism is at the other end of the scale. Long closed to the outside world because of geography and political policy, Bhutan has only allowed air travel since 1974.

When the country was opened to tourists, the rulers set out to retain the Kingdom's unique culture and traditions by only allowing for small numbers of very controlled tourism developments, mainly catering to a limited number of higher-income visitors. Additionally, visitors must go through one of the limited number of licensed Bhutanese tour operators so more of the revenue will stay within the country.

Travel to such an exotic and remote destination has become popular in recent years and pressures have been mounting. For now, the policy of restricting tourism to keep the environmental and cultural impact minimal appears to be working though.

VOCABULARY

Here are some words that will be useful in this unit. How many do you know? Work with a partner to figure out the meaning of any words that you don't know.

all in one	have an impact on	revenue leakage
activity supplements	infrastructure	shortages
the other end of the scale	isolate	strain
exclusive tour	mountain trek	sustainable tourism
extinction	natural resources	traditional
fragile economy	paradise	vacation package

What other words and phrases do you know related to the topic?

VOCABULARY ACTIVITIES

A. Read each definition. Fill in the blank with the opposite word or phrase from the list above. Remember to use the correct word form.

1. mass tourism _____
2. robust business and healthy government _____
3. hellish _____
4. man made products _____
5. surpluses _____
6. individualized travel _____
7. money coming into the economy _____
8. large, healthy population _____
9. to be surrounded _____
10. to have no effect _____

B. Write sentences using ten of the words or phrases above. Work with a partner to compare your sentences.

GRAPHIC ORGANIZER

Consider the positive or negative effects of tourism. Complete the table. Work with a partner. Compare your answers.

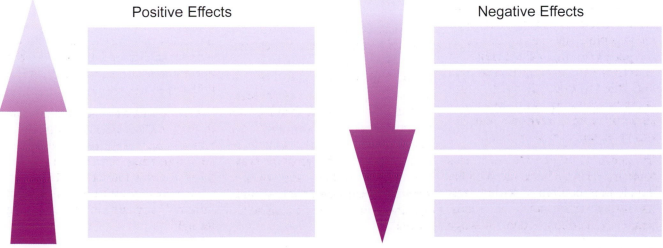

Positive Effects

Negative Effects

PRE-LISTENING QUESTIONS

1. Think of a tourist development you know well. What is it like?
2. Has the overall impact of the development been positive or negative for the local people? For the environment? For tourists?

SITUATION: *Jenny and Ryan are discussing a new tourist resort.*

Jenny	It's so calm and peaceful. It's really lovely here, isn't it?
Ryan	Yeah, and it'll be even better next year. They're planning to build a new tourist resort over on the other side of the lake.
Jenny	Excuse me, but how can you say that's a good thing?
Ryan	It'll be a wonderful place to stay and more people will get to really enjoy the lake. They'll have boats, windsurfers, a supervised beach, waterslides, and great facilities like a spa, a super restaurant, and even a small casino.
Jenny	Don't you think that building such facilities will destroy everything that brings people here in the first place? It won't be very peaceful if it's full of motor boats, will it?
Ryan	It's a big lake, and it can absorb that kind of activity. There's nowhere to stay around here that's very nice.
Jenny	But you have to accept that you can't have nature and tranquility with a huge resort around you.
Ryan	I think you're mistaken. If it's done sensitively, the two things can go hand in hand. Haven't you heard about sustainable tourism?
Jenny	Yeah, but that soon disappears when it comes to the bottom line. Do you think that the local community really wants to be overrun with tourists from the city?
Ryan	The local people have been struggling to make a living here for years and the younger ones are leaving. I think most people would really welcome a development like this.
Jenny	Just because tourists come to an area, doesn't mean that the money will stay here, though. A lot would go to the owners of the development. And what about the roads? They're in a terrible state now.
Ryan	Well that's the advantage of the new development. They're going to contribute to building new roads. That'll help both locals and tourists.
Jenny	I just think things like the new roads will do more harm than good.

CHECK FOR UNDERSTANDING

1. What kind of new development is being planned?
2. What kind of things does Jenny worry about?
3. What does Ryan see as the advantages?
4. Why have young people been leaving?
5. Why are developments like this a compromise?

Work with a partner. Compare your answers.

Quick Fact
According to UN figures, tourists spend more than $2 billion each day.

PRACTICE AND DISCUSSION

PERSONALIZATION

Complete these sentences with your own ideas.

If people plan a new resort, they should think about...

Tourism is/isn't necessarily...

Tourism can be ... for a community.

Tourists do/don't have a responsibility to...

Now share your sentences with a classmate.

DISCUSSION STRATEGIES - Asking critical questions

When discussing an issue or situation, sometimes you disagree with the other person's point of view and you might want to ask a slightly critical question or make an interjection in order to point out the weaknesses in her/his argument. Here are some ways of doing this:

How can you say...?

You have to accept...

What about...?

Don't you think...?

I think you're mistaken...

What makes you so sure...?

You can also use question tags e.g. **..., isn't it?**

Think of more examples.

Discussion Strategy in Action

Listen to the conversations. Write down the question and the point of view of the person asking the question.

Question	Point of view
1. _____	_____
_____	_____
2. _____	_____
_____	_____
3. _____	_____
_____	_____

Discussion Practice

Work with a partner. Discuss these statements using the critical questioning strategies above.

1. Tourism really helps economically deprived areas.
2. Developing new transport infrastructure, such as roads or cheap flight services, helps bring tourism to isolated areas.
3. When tourism comes to an area, everyone benefits.
4. Tourism can help promote the protection of endangered species by allowing more people to see animals in the wild.

FURTHER ACTIVITIES

ROLE PLAY

> **Brainstorming:**
>
> What are the social and environmental consequences of tourism?
> What possible impact could tourism have on the local community?

A new tourist resort is going to open in an area of great beauty. The area is also well known for the small communities of people who maintain the cultural traditions and live in a way that has remained unchanged for many years.

Work with a partner. One person plays the role of a resort developer who wants to convince the local community of your company's good intentions. The second person is a local community leader who is anxious to encourage new developments, but also wants any development to be very sensitive to the unique environment and the way of life of the local population.

Discuss the implications of the new resort. Consider ways to maximize the benefits and make suggestions for minimizing any environmental damage and anything that will disturb the local population.

ACTIVITY

Work with a partner. Make a list of the jobs different kinds of tourism can create.

Consider the following:

- Travel to and from a destination
- Travel while at a destination
- Food, lodging
- Attractions, events, activities
- Advertising
- Resources

Choose one of the jobs. Work with a partner. Describe the job. Include how it could be carried out with maximum sensitivity to the environment and the local community.

SPEECHES - A new development model that works

An international hotel chain wants to build a resort in an environmentally sensitive area. It is important to develop the area and you want to make sure that this is the right kind of development.

Give a speech as part of a debate with the developers and the local planners. Consider the following:

- What is special about the area and needs to be protected.
- How big the development should be.
- How it would affect local infrastructures.
- How the community could be more involved.
- How you can protect the local environment and natural resources.
- How the effects of the development can be monitored.
- Ways of working together to find a solution that works for everyone.

Give your speech to a group of students who are playing the roles of hotel developers and local planners. They should critically question you afterwards and engage in debate.

CONSOLIDATION AND RECYCLING

BUILDING VOCABULARY

Fill in the blanks.

Ten years ago, low-cost vacation 1._____ were encouraging too many people to come to this island. It became over- 2._____ and unpleasant. It soon lost its popularity. More and more people started looking at going on different types of vacations such as 3._____ tours, 4._____ trekking, and 5._____ tourism. However, recently the 6._____ economy really improved when investors opened up a new golf and conference center. On the downside, as a result of the huge complex going up, there is a shortage of a lot of the 7._____ resources of the island such as wood and fresh water.

WRITING

Write a marketing brochure for a new, sustainable tourist resort. The resort has been designed to be environmentally friendly and the company running the development works in cooperation with the local community.

As you plan your brochure, consider the following:

- Where it is and why people would want to go there.
- What kind of people you want to attract and how you would do it.
- How expensive it is e.g. if it is more expensive than other types of resorts, how can you justify the cost and make it more attractive to the tourists?
- What impact it will have on the local environment and how to make this into a marketing feature.
- What impact it will have on the local community, how to involve them positively in the resort, and how to make this into a marketing feature.
- What key features enable it to work as a 'sustainable resort'?

Show your brochure to your classmates and ask for their feedback. What do they think works best in the brochure? What is less successful?

REFLECTION

1. How responsible do you feel you are for the impact you have as a traveler? Think of examples, and discuss them with your group.

2. Do tourists have a big impact on your community? Think of some examples and discuss them with your group.

3. Would you pay more to stay in a resort hotel that is "environmentally friendly"?

Media Violence

Violence. Is it the price of freedom?

Last week we wrote that the violence in Louis Haytall's movies has reached an unacceptable level. Many of our readers wrote in to agree and several even suggested his movies should be banned. Here, we give him a chance to reply to the criticism.

There is a lot of talk about violence in the media these days and much of it is directed towards my movies.

In my opinion, violence is part of modern day movie-making and it is up to the viewers to decide what they want to see. There are plenty of classic movies that contain horrible violence but no one complains about them. Think about *Schindler's list*, *Apocalypse now,* or even *Gone with the wind*!

Let's face it, violence surrounds us in more than just movies. Look at the news – you can't get more violent than that and it's real. And don't forget about all the violence you can find in books, computer games, some manga cartoons, and even in music, just look at the lyrics of any gangsta rap. Why should movies be singled out for criticism? Each country has a classification system and as long as viewers can clearly see what kind of movie it is, they should be able to choose what to watch. You don't need to censor things, you just need to inform people and give them choices.

A lot of critics say that my movies are unsuitable for children. They highlight studies that show the high number of violent acts a child will see each year and suggest this is harmful. However, they omit to say that children cannot see my movies at the cinema. Most of the violence children see is in TV programs, cartoons even; things that parents could easily stop their children from seeing if they so wished.

I have never found any convincing evidence to support the argument that watching violence in movies or TV programs increases violent behavior in society. Violence was part of life long before the media became such an integral part of our daily lives. I believe that violence in the media helps vent this kind of aggression so society is actually more peaceful now than it would otherwise be. Countries like Japan have lots of violence in the different media yet maintain low crime rates.

There have been a few copycat acts inspired by scenes from violence in movies. But even here, there is no proven link between the acts and movies. Those people may have committed similar crimes anyway. They are obviously disturbed individuals.

I understand that my movies may offend some people, but my DVD sales indicate that an awful lot of people do like them. I just want the freedom to produce the kinds of movies that interest and entertain lots of people. People have the freedom to choose not to watch them.

VOCABULARY

Here are some words that will be useful in this unit. How many do you know?
Work with a partner to figure out the meaning of any words that you don't know.

ban	disturb	offensive
censorship	fantasy	right
classification	freedom	torture
complaints	gratuitous	violence
cruelty	images	witness

What other words and phrases do you know related to the topic?

VOCABULARY ACTIVITIES

A. Complete with forms of the words from the list. Remember to use the correct word form.

Many parents are 1._____ by the level of violence in computer games. The concern is that in a lot of video games the children participate more actively in shooting or acts of 2._____. Many parents and educators are worried about the psychological effect of this. Children who 3._____ excess violence from a young age become desensitized to it and have trouble differentiating 4._____ from reality. Some researchers claim that there is a link between violent computer games and 5._____. Many people 6. _____ about excessively violent computer games and would like to see them 7. _____ altogether. They dismiss the argument about 8. _____ of expression because they think that the games manufacturers don't respect the rights of children to be brought up in a healthy and safe environment.

B. Suggest at least three examples from the different types of media for each of the following points. Work with a partner. Compare and discuss your choices.

1. gratuitous violence
2. classification systems
3. offensive images or text
4. cruelty

GRAPHIC ORGANIZER

Complete the chart with examples of movies or TV programs that you think are acceptable and unacceptable to most viewers. Work with a partner. Compare your ideas.

MOVIE	LEVEL OF VIOLENCE			
	unacceptable	depends on age	acceptable	unsure

POINTS OF VIEW *PC games are too violent.*

PRE-LISTENING QUESTIONS

1. Can you think of areas in which censorship of violent computer games can be helpful?
2. What sort of limits would you impose?

Track 9

SITUATION: *Craig and Alison are discussing a violent game.*

Craig	I just got Hell's Enemy IV – it's supposed to be even better than the last one. I can't wait to get home and play it.
Alison	Isn't that the game that caused such a stir about torture and extreme cruelty?
Craig	Yeah, but that's just one part of the game.
Alison	You mean torture is okay as long as it's just part of a game?
Craig	What I mean is that there are lots of other really cool elements to this game. Sure, there are scenes of torture, but it's just fantasy. On this latest version of the game the graphics are supposed to be amazing.
Alison	Wait, am I hearing you correctly? You're saying that it's all right to show cruelty and torture as a form of entertainment as long as it's done with good graphics?
Craig	Of course not. But, hello, violent images are everywhere in our culture. This is just a game and a bit of violence gives it an extra edge. It makes it more realistic.
Alison	What about the fact that so much of the violence is directed towards women? I always thought you were so careful about that sort of thing. I can't really get my head around this new you.
Craig	Oh give me a break – you watch horror flicks. I mean, what can be more gruesome than a vampire sucking people's blood. I think you're being a bit hypocritical.
Alison	Come off it – there's a big difference between being scared by something in a movie and actively participating in it in a game.
Craig	Either way – there's a sort of thrill involved with it, isn't there?
Alison	No. Even pretending to torture someone is just sick and by buying into that you're supporting a sick part of society and maybe even in danger of becoming part of it.
Craig	Alison, we're talking about a computer game, not World War III!
Alison	You need to think a little more carefully about the sorts of products you support.
Craig	And you need to get real.

Quick Fact
In 2007, a video game banned in the U.K., but released in the U.S.A. with an 'M' (mature) rating contained 'AO' (adults only) rated material that could be unlocked with a code circulated on the Internet.

CHECK FOR UNDERSTANDING

1. What does Alison watch that contains violence? Why does she think it's acceptable?
2. Why does Alison's view of Craig change?
3. Why does Alison think that a violent video game is worse than a horror movie?

Work with a partner. Compare your answers.

PRACTICE AND DISCUSSION

PERSONALIZATION

Complete these sentences with your own ideas.

> *Excuse me, but I think that there's a big difference between ... and...*
>
> *Either way, movies are too...*
>
> *What I mean is, even books can be...*
>
> *You need to ... when buying video games for children.*

Now share your sentences with a classmate.

DISCUSSION STRATEGIES - Asking for clarification

Listed below are a few ways that we can ask for clarification and confirmation in a discussion.

I understand that/It's my understanding that...

Do you mean that... ?

Is/Isn't that... ?

Do you believe that... ?

Are you saying/suggesting that... ?

Am I hearing you correctly?

It is true that...

You're implying that...

Think of more examples.

Discussion Strategy in Action

Listen to the conversations. For each one, answer the following questions:

- What is the initial statement?
- What expression does the speaker use to ask for clarification?
- What is the initial speaker's main idea?

1. initial statement   _____
   asking for clarification   _____
   main idea   _____

2. initial statement   _____
   asking for clarification   _____
   main idea   _____

3. initial statement   _____
   asking for clarification   _____
   main idea   _____

Discussion Practice

Work with a partner. Discuss the following statements. Use the discussion strategies.

1. Violent cartoons can be harmful to children. They should be banned.
2. It's okay if people want to watch violence on TV as long as they don't act violently.
3. The way women are presented in the media is getting worse. They are often victims of violence.
4. People need violence in the media. It helps them to get rid of their frustrations.

ROLE PLAY

> **Brainstorming:**
> What kinds of things in movies might people find offensive?
> How can you choose a broad range of movies without offending anyone?
> What is acceptable and unacceptable in movies for young adults?

You are on a committee putting together a student movie festival. Two of the movies are very interesting but also violent and potentially offensive to women.
Consider the following:

- Most of the people going to see the movies will be students from a wide range of backgrounds. Some are particularly concerned about violence against women in movies.
- Both movies claim to be against violence and crime, but they say that they need to show the harm in it in order to make their points.
- The makers of the movies are students who are very talented and this might give them a big break. If their movies are not accepted it will be difficult for them to get them shown in other places.
- One of the main aims of the festival is to give alternative movie makers an opportunity to show their movies.

Work with a partner. One person will represent a group campaigning against violence in the media. The other person will play the role of a member of the selection committee who thinks that it is important to show them. Discuss the situation.

ACTIVITY

Work with a partner. Propose a set of guidelines about acceptable levels of violence on TV.
Consider the following:

- Real violence e.g. the news.
- The sensitivity of younger or older viewers.
- Different types of programs.
- If there are times which are more appropriate for showing and promoting violent programs.
- Warnings about violence that can go on before the program.

SPEECHES - A book festival

Choose one situation.

1. Give a talk at a book festival presenting a new series of manga style books. You need to give an enthusiastic presentation, but also warn the audience that some of the books might be a little violent for young teens. Explain why you think the violence is acceptable in this case.

2. Give a talk that opens a book festival. You need to give an enthusiastic presentation, but also need to announce that you have decided to ban certain types of manga books from the festival. You need to give your reasons and justifications for this.

Consider the following:

- Set a tone for the whole festival/your new series of books.
- Build up enthusiasm for the new manga books that will be appearing.
- Deal with the issue of censorship in a way which will satisfy most people.
- Clearly explain your position (as a book publisher/festival organizer) in regards to the above.

Present your speech and discuss any questions the audience might have.

CONSOLIDATION AND RECYCLING

BUILDING VOCABULARY

A. We often use language full of imagery. This can be especially common in informal language. Match the expressions to their meaning:

When we say:	We mean:
1. get real	a. created controversy
2. this gives it an extra edge	b. don't be ridiculous
3. I can't really get my head around this	c. makes something more exciting
4. oh give me a break	d. don't be so naïve
5. caused a stir	e. I can't understand/accept this

B. Work with a partner. Take turns making appropriate sentences with the above expressions. Your partner must tell you if they think it sounds natural or not.

C. See how many other expressions with images you can find.

WRITING

Write a review of a violent film, TV program, book or computer game you have seen. Include the following things:

- Describe the kind of violence and the level of it.
- Clearly state if you think that the level of violence is acceptable or not and give your reasons.
- Conclude by saying who you think it would be suitable for (if anyone) and if it has been marketed and classified in the correct way.

Work in a group. Read your reviews. Comment on each person's review to see how many people share the same point of view.

REFLECTION

What do you think about violence as entertainment?

1. Is it acceptable in all forms?
2. Do you think that it influences people? How?
3. Would you be in favour of greater or lesser controls over it?

Quick Fact
By the time the average American child is 18 years old, he or she will witness on television approximately 200,000 acts of violence including 40,000 murders. (Huston et al, 1992)

Body Image

The fashion industry has often been criticized for promoting a dangerously thin body image. These complaints intensified when the deaths of three well known and popular young models were linked to eating disorders. Luisel Ramos died during a fashion show in August 2006. A few months later, Ana Carolina Reston died and then in February 2007, less than five months after Luisel's death, her sister Eliana died. She was only 18 years old.

Designers, retailers, manufacturers, modeling agencies, and the media have all been accused of promoting super slim, 'size zero' models. The prominent use of such unnaturally thin models, it is argued, leads to an increase in eating disorders such as bulimia and anorexia nervosa even among models.

When Luisel Ramos died, the 1.7m (5'9") tall model weighed only 44 kg (98 lbs) giving her a Body Mass Index (BMI) of only 15 (kg/m^2). Anything less than 16 is considered severely thin by the World Health Organization (WHO).

Organizations in some countries have tried to ban models with a BMI of less than 18. But how much will really change when we live in a society that is increasingly obsessed with having a certain look and how much responsibility should the fashion industry accept when they are reacting to market demand – thin, 'perfectly' proportioned models help sell clothes, accessories, and magazines?

Young people tend to be very susceptible. Media and peer pressure have a strong influence on what these impressionable youths think they should look like. It is increasingly common for even young children to go on quick-weight-loss diets, but dieting to lose weight quickly is not the same as following a healthy diet on a permanent basis.

Meanwhile, being extremely overweight or obese is also an issue that needs to be addressed sensitively. There are very serious health problems with obesity which is already common in high-income countries and is becoming increasingly serious in other countries, particularly in urban areas. People just don't get as much exercise as they used to and they are eating more high-fat and sugary foods.

People around the world are also becoming increasingly dissatisfied with other aspects of their appearance too, thinking for example that their nose is too long or their chin is two narrow. Many are turning to plastic surgery to give them the 'right' face and body by enhancements, reductions, or implants. The trend may have started in the U.S.A., but demand for instant transformation is international. China is just one country where plastic surgery is booming and is already a multi-million dollar industry.

This focus on exterior appearance can affect how we feel and how we act, as well as how others act towards us. Many people acknowledge that this is not right, but it is difficult to fight against something that is so pervasive – it is everywhere we look.

VOCABULARY

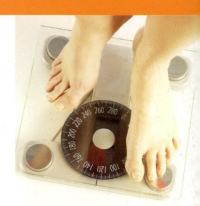

Here are some words that will be useful in this unit. How many do you know? Work with a partner to figure out the meaning of any words that you don't know.

anorexic / anorexia	liposuction	reduction
bulimic / bulimia	obese / obesity	sedentary
crash diets	obsess / obsessive	stunning
dissatisfied	overweight	susceptible
enhanced / enhancement	positive / negative body image	unattainable

What other words and phrases do you know related to the topic?

VOCABULARY ACTIVITIES

A. Write the opposites.

achievable	_____	overconfident	_____
content	_____	overweight	_____
enhancement	_____	unattractive	_____
natural	_____	very active	_____

B. Work with a partner. Take turns making sentences about the illustration in the Graphic Organizer below. Your partner will then make a statement using the opposite of the words or expressions.

GRAPHIC ORGANIZER

Create a mind map about extreme body shapes. Work with a partner. Compare your ideas.

Underweight

health problems

psychological & social problems

causes

Overweight

health problems

psychological & social problems

causes

PRE-LISTENING QUESTIONS

1. Do you think that dieting is a good idea?
2. Do you know anyone who diets or exercises excessively?

SITUATION: *Janine and Chris are discussing dieting.*

Janine	I can't get into my favorite jeans anymore. It's really depressing. I'm going on a diet.
Chris	Well I think you look fine. You shouldn't worry about it.
Janine	Are you kidding? Being overweight is a huge disadvantage, especially for women. People think you're a real loser: they insult you; it's difficult to find nice clothes; and sometimes it's even a barrier to getting a job.
Chris	All right, that may be true if you're really obese, but you're only slightly overweight.
Janine	You see, you do think I'm fat. Now, I'm definitely going to go on a crash diet, something that'll work quickly. There's a new one in this magazine.

Chris	That's crazy. Don't you know that most diets are fads and don't work? Within a few months something like 95 percent of people have put the weight back on.
Janine	Well, I could always go for liposuction.
Chris	That is just so disgusting. I can't believe you're even joking about something like that. You are joking aren't you?
Janine	Sure. Well, I can't afford it anyway. It is becoming more popular though. Just look at the number of ads in this magazine.
Chris	I'm so sick of seeing plastic surgery ads everywhere. They make people think that liposuction, a new nose, or bigger lips will suddenly solve all their problems.
Janine	Well, you work out in the gym!
Chris	Yeah, but that's for general health and fitness.
Janine	Sure, part of it is. But it's also to build up your muscles so you look better. Go on, admit it.
Chris	Maybe. I'm not saying it's wrong to want to look good, but I do think that being obsessed with your appearance is a problem.
Janine	And all I'm saying is that I'd like to lose a little weight.
Chris	Okay, I'll tell you what, why don't we go and play tennis this afternoon?
Janine	That's a great idea and afterwards we can go for pizza.

Quick Fact
Breast reduction surgery is the fifth most common surgical procedure among men in the U.S.A.
– Newsweek 2007

CHECK FOR UNDERSTANDING

1. Why does Janine think it's important to lose weight?
2. What are the different ways of losing weight that are mentioned in the conversation?
3. Why does Chris object to ads for plastic surgery?
4. Why does Chris work out in the gym?
5. Why does Chris think it's dangerous to become too obsessed with body image?

Work with a partner. Compare your answers.

PRACTICE AND DISCUSSION

PERSONALIZATION

Complete these sentences with your own ideas.

I'm not saying it's wrong to look good, but…

I wouldn't touch … for anything in the world.

I'm definitely going to…

I can't believe that people would…

All I'm saying is…

Now share your sentences with a classmate.

DISCUSSION STRATEGIES - Taking exception in a casual context

Listed below are a few ways that we can disagree with a friend in a casual context (they are less appropriate for more formal situations). How many more can you think of?

Well I think that…	**You don't honestly think…**
All right, that may be true, but…	**That's crazy/insane/stupid/ridiculous.**
I'm not saying… but…	**I can't believe you think that…**
No way…	**Give me a break…**
Are you kidding/serious?	**You've got to be kidding.**

Think of more examples.

Discussion Strategy in Action

Listen to the conversations. For each one, answer the following questions:

- What is the main idea in the initial statement?
- What expression does the second speaker use to take exception?

	Initial Statement	Expression Used
1.	_____	_____
2.	_____	_____
3.	_____	_____
4.	_____	_____

Discussion Practice

Work with a partner. How would you respond if a friend said these things?

1. Being so heavy is almost like being handicapped.
2. Most girls will want plastic surgery at some point in their lives.
3. Men don't/can't understand the pressures on women to look good.
4. Men are under pressure to spend a lot of time and money on their looks.
5. It's pointless trying to change the way you look. Be satisfied with the way you are.

FURTHER ACTIVITIES

ROLE PLAY

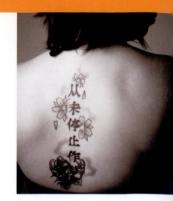

> **Brainstorming:**
>
> What kinds of things do people dislike about their appearance?
>
> What might they do to change their appearance? Should they?
>
> What are the health/personal consequences of changes in appearance?
>
> What kind of advice might be useful? Who can give this advice?

Work with a partner. You don't like something about your body and seek advice from a friend. As a close friend, your partner will listen and discuss your concerns with you. Take turns playing each role. Use expressions from the discussion strategies where possible.

Concerns:

- You think you are too thin and look weak and unhealthy. You need to gain weight in order to be more attractive, but it's very difficult for you. You might be suffering from a bigger health problem.

- You have a large tattoo that you would like to have removed. It will be quite a serious operation and there will always be a scar.

- You think you are overweight. You are extremely self-conscious about this. Actually you are only a little overweight, but you do have some bad eating habits and you don't exercise properly. You have been on about 10 different diets in the last few years. Nothing seems to work. You have just read about a new crash diet in which you can lose two kilos in a week.

- You have a birth mark on your face. You are very attractive, but the mark bothers you so you want to have an operation to get it removed. It will be quite a serious operation. There are risks and the surgery will cost a lot of money.

ACTIVITY

Complete the questionnaire on page 98. Then work with a partner and compare your answers. What do your partner's answers tell you about how they feel about their appearance?

SPEECHES - Being positive about your body

Imagine that you have to give an informal talk about positive body images to a group of teenagers. What kind of message would you like to get through to them? Be careful, you don't want them to be too critical of their own bodies or their friends.

Consider the following:

- Peer and external (media) pressure.
- The importance of being confident about yourself.
- Ways of coping with criticism.
- Having a healthy, balanced diet, lifestyle etc.

Give your talk to a group of students from your class who will role play being teenagers. Respond to any questions they may have as they come up or at the end of the talk.

CONSOLIDATION AND RECYCLING

BUILDING VOCABULARY

A. Words can take different forms in different contexts. Choose the correct form of the words below to complete the dialog.

obsess	anorexia	pretty	health
stun	dietary	dissatisfy	attain

A: I'm not so sure about Julia's new look. I think she looked much 1. _____ before.

B: I don't agree. I think she looks 2. _____

A: You can't be serious. The surgery is so obvious and she's lost way too much weight. Her legs and arms are so thin that she looks 3. _____ .

B: Would you prefer her to stay overweight?

A: She was only a little overweight. I just think that she doesn't take a very 4. _____ approach to her lifestyle. She thinks that a quick fix 5. _____ and cosmetic surgery are the answer to everything.

B: Well at least she's happy with the way she looks. She used to be 6. _____ every time she looked in the mirror. You surely agree that her nose looks better now.

A: She may be happy now, but it won't be long before she develops an 7. _____ with another part of her body. She's looking for perfection and we both know that's 8. _____ .

B. Write new sentences using another form of the words in the box above.

WRITING

Choose two of the situations below and write a letter to the editor of a magazine or paper. Then work with a partner. Exchange your letters and write a reply as though you are the magazine's editor.

- There are many photos taken at a fashion show that only show very young and thin models.
- There was an article in the magazine promoting skin lightening products.
- There are lots of adverts in the magazine for cosmetic surgery. The adverts are aimed primarily at very young people.
- Yet another fad diet is being promoted.
- Only perfect and very glamorous people are featured in the magazine.

REFLECTION

Have a class discussion about body image in your country:

1. How has it changed over the last few years?
2. Is it more or less important than five years ago?
3. What sort of pressures exist to conform to a certain body/face shape?

Cybersafe?

Is cyberspace safe?

Gerry McCall (not his real name), used to be a computer programmer. He is now banned from using computers because he was a persistent hacker. He repeatedly hacked into U.S. military computer networks, but claimed that he only did so to find out more about the Pentagon's UFO files. McCall may have just been a computer geek with too much time on his hands and may not have done anything to directly threaten the security of the U.S.A., but his actions did highlight the potential for serious security threats and made the U.S. government realize how vulnerable their systems were.

Countries and organizations are quickly waking up to the threat from professional cybercriminals and amateur hackers. Malicious viruses can cripple systems and wipe out information. Governments and companies are increasingly worried about the threat of cybercrime. They are afraid of enemies hacking into their systems and spying, sabotaging, or wiping out their systems. The potential for damage is huge.

Criminals, especially those involved with organized crime syndicates, can afford to hire highly skilled people to carry out illegal acts such as fraud, money laundering, and the distribution of illegal downloads. The problem with these crimes is that they go beyond borders and laws and the ability to detect them and make arrests varies between each country. Many countries are working together to devise new international laws and agreements in order to catch and prosecute particularly horrible crimes such as child pornography and its distribution, but the criminals often keep one step ahead.

Many people enjoy using the Internet, but individuals are also in danger of being 'attacked' by viruses which can wipe out computers, or phishing (a type of identity theft where thieves get access to other people's bank accounts in order to steal from them). Other, more vicious, attacks against vulnerable people include being 'stalked' by people met in chat rooms.

This is not to mention activities such as illegal downloading of music and movies, downloading school or university coursework, and slander. Policing the Internet is a huge and difficult job which requires levels of cooperation which do not exist, not to mention enormous levels of funding. The range and seriousness of crimes committed on the Internet tend to make McCall's offense seem a little less serious. However, many governments are determined to treat all cybercrime severely. When you think of the potential for damage, this is understandable. As new technologies, such as mobile phone Internet access evolve, so does the work of the cybercriminals.

We shouldn't forget what a wonderful tool the Internet is when used with the right precautions. Many people have become so dependent on the Internet for work, education, communications, shopping, and even their social life that they just could not imagine doing without it.

VOCABULARY

Here are some words that will be useful in this unit. How many do you know? Work with a partner to figure out the meaning of any words that you don't know.

anti-spyware	firewall	PIN number
anti-virus	geek	phishing
chat room	hack into	to access
computer virus	hacker	to input
cyberterrorism	illegal downloads	wipe out

What other words and phrases do you know related to the topic?

VOCABULARY ACTIVITIES

A.   Match the words above with the correct definition below.

1._____ A program that gains access to your computer with the intent of damaging it or allowing others to access it.

2._____ Using the Internet to spy, sabotage, or destroy other systems for political reasons.

3._____ Personal identification number – used for accessing files, programs or accounts.

4._____ A website where unacquainted people can exchange messages with each other.

5._____ Sending messages to people so that they give their bank and PIN details.

6._____ To enter information or programs into computers.

7._____ To be able to get information or files.

8._____ Program that stops spyware from tracking information on your computer.

B.   Write definitions for the remaining vocabulary above. Work with a partner and compare your definitions.

1._____   -   _____

2._____   -   _____

3._____   -   _____

4._____   -   _____

5._____   -   _____

6._____   -   _____

7._____   -   _____

GRAPHIC ORGANIZER

Provide examples of different uses of the Internet. They may be positive, negative, or potentially both. Work with a partner. Compare your ideas.

NEGATIVE   **POSITIVE**

POINTS OF VIEW *It's too dangerous to use the Internet.*

PRE-LISTENING QUESTIONS

1. What precautions do you take when you use the Internet?
2. What are the dangers you face in using the Internet?

SITUATION: *Mark and Emma are discussing the risks involved in using the Internet.*

Mark	I'm so stressed out. I just lost my whole term paper because my computer had a virus. It completely wiped out my hard drive.
Emma	Didn't you have any virus protection?
Mark	I did, but it was out of date. I guess it's partly my fault.
Emma	I think it's so risky using the Internet these days.
Mark	That's a bit of an overreaction.
Emma	No, it isn't. The Internet is a dangerous place. For example, did you know that if a hacker really wants to get into your computer, he can access all your files as well as your Internet transactions? That means all of your personal information, including credit card transactions can be hacked into.
Mark	That may be true if you're not careful, but you can take steps to avoid it such as keeping your virus protection up to date and installing a really good firewall.
Emma	But there's no absolute guarantee. Look what just happened to you. And take my uncle; his company had up-to-date anti-spyware and everything, but an employee leaving the company copied files about their new technology, then he went to another firm pretending that it was his. My uncle couldn't prove a thing.
Mark	All that proves is that people are dishonest. It's nothing to do with computers.
Emma	But computers make it easier for people to commit crimes like that. Look at online banking.
Mark	Well, yes, banking is a good example. Even if you don't want to bank through your computer, your bank uses computers all the time and thieves can get access to your account details that way.
Emma	Yes, but if you use the Internet for banking and buying things less frequently, your chances of having problems are reduced.
Mark	That's just not practical in today's world. Look at the person who lives in a small town where there are few specialty stores. There are a lot of things you simply can't find there. More stores only operate online these days and they say that's a trend that is going to increase.
Emma	I still think it's too risky.
Mark	And I don't know what I would do without the Internet.

✓ CHECK FOR UNDERSTANDING

1. Why didn't Mark's anti-virus protection work?
2. Why does Emma not like using the Internet?
3. Why does Mark think that she's being too cautious?
4. What happened to Emma's uncle?
5. Why is the Internet useful to people living in a small town?

Work with a partner. Compare your answers.

Quick Fact
Three hundred online crimes were carried out every hour in the U.K. in 2006, but 90% went unreported.
- 1871 Ltd for Garlik

PRACTICE AND DISCUSSION

PERSONALIZATION

Complete these sentences with your own ideas.

The Internet is a dangerous place, for example,…

You can take steps to avoid problems with the Internet such as…

There's no absolute guarantee of Internet safety, take…

…is a good example of how computers make it easier to commit crimes.

There are many ways of being careful when using a computer such as…

Now share your sentences with a classmate.

DISCUSSION STRATEGIES - Giving examples or supporting statements

In a discussion, your arguments will carry a lot more weight if they are backed up by facts or examples. Below are a few expressions to help introduce them:

For example, …	**Take…**
Look at…	**Did you know/realize that…?**
Such as/like…	**Another reason…**

Think of more examples.

Discussion Strategy in Action

Listen to the conversations. For each one, note the example of a supporting statement.

Conversation	Supporting Statement
1.	_____
2.	_____
3.	_____
4.	_____

Discussion Practice

Work with a partner. Create short dialogs based on the statements below.
Use the expressions above to support your points.

1. Cybercrime is very difficult to act against.
2. There are many ways to protect yourself against cybercrime.
3. Some people think that hacking is just a bit of fun.
4. You need to be careful about giving out personal information online.
5. We get most of our information through the Internet now.

FURTHER ACTIVITIES

ROLE PLAY

Work with a partner. You are not careful enough with your use of the Internet. Your friend is concerned and tries to convince you to change the way you do the following things online:

Brainstorming:

Think about things that you like to do online. What are the potential dangers?

- gambling
- going into chat rooms, giving out personal information, and meeting people
- downloading movies and music illegally
- spending too much time online in chat rooms, playing games, and never seeing people and socializing
- downloading essays and submitting them as your own work

ACTIVITY

Work with a partner. Choose one of the topics below.

- online chat rooms and instant messaging
- general email use
- downloading files
- surfing the Web
- online banking
- buying things online

Provide guidance on carrying on the activity safely. Consider the following:

Who you want to give the advice to.

The best way to get the information to the target audience.

The risks they face when they go online.

How they can be safer online.

Research you need to carry out to on your topic – how it operates, what the dangers are, examples of problems encountered, and steps that can be taken to prevent them.

SPEECHES - A presentation on Internet safety

Choose a different topic from the list above. Give a practical presentation to the class about your subject. Include some general tips on how to use the Internet safely.

- Remember to give lots of information and examples
- You might want to present an information sheet to go with it, for example,
  - list useful websites,
  - sites to be wary of
  - blockers for certain sites, pop up ads, spam, and phishing

Hold a question and answer session at the end.

CONSOLIDATION AND RECYCLING

BUILDING VOCABULARY

Expressions related to computers can be confusing. Choose the correct word or phrase from those listed below to complete the dialog. Remember to use the correct word form.

program	hack	virus	firewall
online	offline	chat room	download
pshishing	access	wipe out	password

A: I don't know what to do. My computer got a virus and now all my files have been 1. _____ .

B: My brother is studying to become a computer 2. _____ . Maybe he can help you. You probably need a good 3. _____ so you can block unwanted programs from 4. _____ your computer.

A: Yeah but does that interfere with your speed? I like to use 5. _____ to communicate with my friends.

B: I don't think it slows things down much at all and you really should have one on. You should actually try to go 6. _____ when you don't need to use the Internet to surf the web.

A: That's a good idea.

B: The other thing you have to be careful of is 7. _____ . My friend sent the details of her bank account, 8. _____ , and PIN number when she got an email she thought was from her bank. Then they took all the money from her account.

A: Don't worry. I never send those kinds of details to people 9. _____ .

WRITING

Many police forces are now hiring ex-hackers to help them solve Internet crime. Write an online advertisement for such a person. Include:

- personal qualities
- experience
- education
- interests
- work conditions

REFLECTION

1. What can you do to make using the Internet safer?
2. Should more be done to protect young people using the Internet?
3. Will cybercrime become easier to detect? Why?

UNIT
6

Modern Families

Extracts from Chelsea's diary:

May 15
I don't want to end up like Mom. She and Dad split up years ago and while he had loads of girlfriends and has remarried, she's had nothing more than the odd date, and some of them have been very weird.

I keep telling Mom that she needs to have a life of her own. Now I'm not so sure. Last week she met a guy at a friend's house. She says that Dave's really nice and funny, but he sounds pretty boring to me. And he's half her age! Anyway she seems a lot happier. Mom hasn't told him that she's got three kids!

May 20
Super stressed out. Supposed to stay with Dad but of course he never came to pick us up. Ever since he married Sherrie, he never shows up when he's supposed to. I don't really care, but Eric and Justin get really upset and I'm the one who has to calm them down.

Mom was ultra upset. She'd planned this romantic dinner for Dave and then had to call it off.

May 30
Love is in the air again. Mom's seeing Dave more and more. The boys aren't too happy about the whole thing because they get a lot less attention – she spoiled them too much before anyway. I have to stay home and baby-sit them but at least Mom's off my back. She's more interested in her wardrobe.

June 30
The big secret is out! Mom told Dave that she has three kids – I guess she's over worrying that he will find out how old she is, too. Anyway, Dave confessed that he's got a little girl. She's six and her name is Britney.

Now we're all supposed to play happy families; starting off with a picnic together!

July 5
The picnic from hell. It started off okay, but on the way to the park, Eric and Justin started hitting each other. Dave turned into some kind of psycho-dad. He shouted at them and he was really scary. We were all totally shocked.

We got to the lake and then Britney started acting up. She's such a little princess: "Daddy, I want this." "Daddy, I don't like that." Dave just jumped every time she opened her little mouth.

It got worse after that. Dave clearly has no idea about how to deal with other people's kids. He even called Eric and Justin a couple of thugs. I just laughed 'cause he sounded like such an idiot. Anyway it ended with Mom telling him to shut up, then they had a big fight.

Mom's pretty upset but I'm glad they've broken up. I like having her to myself again. The boys are so happy, too.

VOCABULARY

Here are some words that will be useful in this unit. How many do you know? Work with a partner to figure out the meaning of any words that you don't know.

adopt	ex-girlfriend/boyfriend	separation
break up	ex-husband/wife	stepfather/mother
common-law partner	father/mother-in-law	stepson/daughter
custody	foster	stepbrother/sister
divorce	halfbrother/sister	support

What other words and phrases do you know related to the topic?

VOCABULARY ACTIVITIES

A. The following text is based on information from the reading on page 36. Complete it using words from the list above. Remember to use the correct word form.

Kathy and Steve are Chelsea's parents. They are 1. _____ so Steve is Kathy's 2. _____ and Kathy is Steve's 3. _____.

Sherrie is Chelsea's 4. _____. Sherrie and Steve have a baby. The baby is called Hugh. Hugh and Chelsea have the same father so Hugh is Chelsea's 5. _____.

Dave has never been married but he lived with a woman called Sue for six years. In the part of Canada where they lived, Sue was regarded as Dave's 6. _____. However, Dave and Sue broke up and they have been 7. _____ for two years.

Sue has 8. _____ of their daughter, but Dave still supports them and he gets to see Britney one weekend each month. If Dave were to marry Kathy, he would be the 9. _____ to her three children and Britney would be Chelsea, Eric and Justin's 10. _____.

B. Work with a partner. Take turns making new sentences to describe the different relationships between the people in activity A above.

Hugh   Britney   Eric   Dave   Steve   Sue   Kathy   Justin

GRAPHIC ORGANIZER

Look at the family tree. Work with a partner. Discuss Justin's relationships. Then draft a tree for your own family.

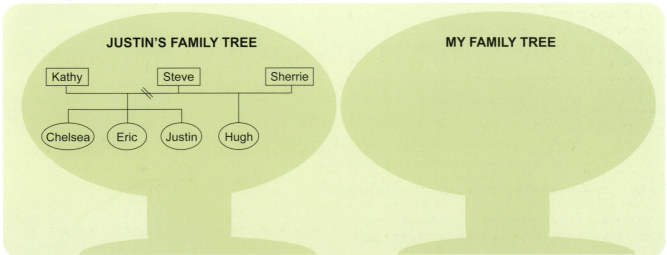

JUSTIN'S FAMILY TREE

MY FAMILY TREE

Kathy — Steve — Sherrie

Chelsea   Eric   Justin   Hugh

POINTS OF VIEW *Divorce is harmful for society.*

PRE-LISTENING QUESTIONS

1. What kinds of problems can divorce cause?
2. How are attitudes towards divorce changing?

SITUATION: *Scott tells and Lin about his family.*

Lin	How was it growing up as a mixed-race child?
Scott	It was never an issue for me, really. I think that any problems I had growing up were more to do with my parents' divorce.
Lin	Is that right?
Scott	Yeah. It wasn't just their race; my parents were from very different social backgrounds, too. My mother's from a wealthy family and my father was poor so that just added to the pressure. There were so many arguments with both sides of the family that they split up when I was eight.
Lin	It can't have been easy for you at such a young age.
Scott	No, it wasn't. And even after they split, they would still fight. They'd usually fight over when my dad could see us so I felt as if I was torn in two – I wanted to see him, but didn't want to upset my mom. And he never made any support payments after he remarried so life was really tough for a while.
Lin	But didn't you say your mother's parents are rich? Wouldn't they help with the finances?
Scott	Yes, they are rich, but even though they didn't approve of the marriage, they don't approve of divorce either so they refused to help out. They'd just say, "We told you so!"
Lin	Wow. That couldn't have been easy for your mom.
Scott	It was terrible. She had to take on extra work and I hardly ever saw her.
Lin	That sounds pretty miserable.
Scott	Oh, I'm not complaining. Luckily we had really nice neighbors, otherwise I'd have ended up in foster care. I think being a single parent was tough on my mother, but it made us very close. My parent's problems probably made me more cautious with close relationships though.

✓ CHECK FOR UNDERSTANDING

1. How does Scott feel about divorce? How do you know?
2. Why did Scott's parents divorce?
3. How did Scott's grandparents react to the divorce?
4. Who raised Scott after his parents divorced?
5. Is Scott close to both his parents now?

Work with a partner. Compare your answers.

Quick Fact
In the U.S.A., the probability of a first marriage ending in separation or divorce within ten years is around 33%.

PRACTICE AND DISCUSSION

PERSONALIZATION

Complete these sentences with your own ideas.

I think that mixed-race marriages…

Fathers should/should not pay to support their families after a divorce because…

I'm sure that couples who divorce too easily…

I guess orphans must feel…

I'm convinced/not convinced that single working mothers…

Children who face conflict in the home…

Children brought up by relatives or siblings…

Now share your sentences with a classmate.

DISCUSSION STRATEGIES - Confirming and prompting for more details

Sometimes in a discussion you want to indicate that you have understood what has been said without interrupting the flow of an interesting conversation. This can often be done by confirming what you have heard and prompting for more information. Listed below are a few ways that we can do this:

Is that right/so?

Yes, I can see/understand…

You must have been/felt…

You really…, don't you? (using question tags)

That couldn't have been…

That sounds…

Think of more examples.

Discussion Strategy in Action

Listen to the conversations. For each one, answer the following questions:
- What is the initial statement?
- How does the listener indicate that he/she had understood and prompt for more information?

Conversation	Initial Statement	Strategy
1		
2		
3		
4		

Discussion Practice

Work with a partner. Using the strategies above, continue the following discussions.

1. I'm tired of being with my girlfriend/boyfriend.
2. I don't think it should be so easy to divorce.
3. Family life today is terrible/great.
4. I would never date someone who already had children.

FURTHER ACTIVITIES

ROLE PLAY

> **Brainstorming:**
>
> What kinds of problems might arise in a modern relationship?
> What kinds of frustrations do men and women face?
> Think of reasons for breaking up and ways of resolving them.

Work with a partner. Take turns acting out each role.

Student 1: You are a relationship counselor and your job is to listen to your client, get to the heart of the problem, and suggest ways of resolving them. Use the discussion strategies in order to extract the relevant information and get more useful details. Finally, summarize the issues and give your advice.

Student 2: You are a young man/woman in a relationship and although you were initially very happy, you are now thinking about ending the relationship.

ACTIVITY

Work with a partner. Look at the pictures and speculate about the different relationships between these people and what you think might happen in the future. Justify your opinions.

SPEECHES - My ideal relationship

Give a short, informal talk to your class about your ideal long-term relationship. Consider the following:

* Would you want to be with the same person for the rest of your life?
* Do you want to get married?
* Do you want to have a child/children?
* Would you hesitate before getting into a close relationship with someone from another culture, background, education, etc.?
* What kind of qualities would you look for in a partner?
* How would you see your relationship working on a day-to-day basis in terms of roles, work, socializing etc.?

Hold a brief question and answer session after your presentation.

CONSOLIDATION AND RECYCLING

BUILDING VOCABULARY

Phrasal verbs are very commonly used in English. They can cause problems because they often have particular meanings. Match the phrasal verbs to the most appropriate meaning.

gang up	get on	meet up	come on	get over
make (it) up	slip off (somewhere)	phone up	call off	pick up
call up	turn (something) around	go out	work out	count on
act up	tell (someone) off	shut up	break up/split up	pull out
show up	make up for	take on	to get away from	get around to

Phrasal Verbs	Meaning:	Phrasal Verbs	Meaning:
_____	to group together to exert pressure	_____	compensate
_____	to relate to each other	_____	get/fetch
_____	get together at a certain time	_____	invent
_____	to finally do something	_____	to cancel
_____	come to terms with something	_____	depend on
_____	to go in an understated way	_____	to telephone
_____	change for the better	_____	avoid or escape
_____	be resolved (for the better usually)	_____	to berate
_____	to end a relationship	_____	to behave improperly

WRITING

Choose one of the following situations. Write a short letter to an advice column giving further details of the problems you face and request help:

- You are a teenage son/daughter and you are very upset because your father has remarried and you can't stand your stepmother or her son.

- You are a young woman with a fantastic career. You are married to a very nice man who doesn't have a very good job. You want to have a baby, but you don't want to stop work. It makes more sense for your husband to stop work and take care of the child, but he won't do this.

- You are a young man/woman and you have met a nice older man/woman with grown up children. You want to have children, but he/she doesn't.

- Your father recently died and you feel your mother should now come and live with you. You know that this will create tensions with your husband/wife.

Work with a partner. Exchange letters then write a reply as the advisor. Summarize the problem then give your advice clearly. Try to offer a couple of alternative solutions.

REFLECTION

1. How has family life changed in the last 20-30 years? What changes have helped society?
2. How do you imagine the trends continuing in the future?
3. Would you rather experience family life as it is today or as it was 20 years ago? Why?

Medicine

How the West is looking East

When professional football players are injured, they might go to their doctor or their physiotherapist, but they're just as likely to visit an acupuncturist. Increasingly in the West, people are turning to alternative forms of medicine and healers. Some people reject Western medicine because they think it only treats the symptoms without looking at the whole person, while others see alternative forms of treatment as complementing Western medicine. These forms range from fairly widely accepted treatments such as acupuncture, some forms of massage, and some other traditional treatments to more controversial treatments such as faith healing and using crystals or magnets to try and cure illness.

In the West the demand for alternative treatments is booming, but it is not without its pitfalls as governments and medical boards struggle to decide what kinds of treatments are safe, which need to be regulated, and which should be covered by national or private health insurance schemes. It is also further confused by treatments which touch on the spiritual wellbeing of the individual in the forms of faith or mystic healing. In Europe, North America and other industrialized regions, it is estimated that over 50 percent of the population has used alternative treatments. It is a growing trend for treatments to combine different types of medical practices. A number of doctors are now getting additional qualifications in areas like acupuncture. Furthermore, herbal treatments, also known as herbal remedies, are a growing commercial market in the West. However, levels of regulation vary widely.

Many of the popular alternative treatments now being practiced in the West have a long history of use in Asia, particularly China and India. Ironically, some Asian doctors are beginning to question the scientific basis for some of the traditional herbal cures.

This fusion of East and West isn't really new. The exchange of medical knowledge has been going on for centuries. It started at least as early as the 17th century when missionaries are known to have brought home knowledge of medicines and techniques they found in Asia. Later, in the 19th century, Western style hospitals and treatments were increasingly being set up in the East. Theories about inoculations that actually started in the East, were often adapted or further developed in the West and have since continued to be refined around the world.

The huge choice of therapies and treatments available can be confusing and unfortunately, not all of them are effective or legitimate. It is difficult and expensive to gather scientific evidence on each one that emerges. However, while some so-called 'healers' have been known to prey on terminally ill victims and families who are desperate to find a cure, there are many treatments that can offer real pain relief, effective treatment, and a safe alternative to invasive treatments which can incur serious side effects.

VOCABULARY

Here are some words that will be useful in this unit. How many do you know? Work with a partner to figure out the meaning of any words that you don't know.

accreditation	heal	life-threatening illness	qualifications
acupuncture	healthcare	mind-body balance	scientific
alternative medicine	herbal treatments	patient	surgery
chronic pain	injury	physiotherapy / therapist	techniques
cure	inoculation	prevention	terminal

What other words and phrases do you know related to the topic?

VOCABULARY ACTIVITIES

A. Circle the sentences where the underlined words are used incorrectly. Replace them with the correct words from the list.

   1. More and more <u>patients</u> are fed up with the limitations of modern medicine.
   2. Many <u>scientists</u> turn to acupuncturists for support.
   3. The man's <u>healing</u> was very serious and he went to the hospital.
   4. Some doctors doubt the <u>inoculation</u> basis for some types of herbal treatment.
   5. A lot of people suffer from <u>chronic pain</u> that never goes away.

B. Work with a partner. Give examples for each of these terms.

   1. alternative medicine
   2. herbal treatment
   3. injury
   4. inoculation
   5. terminal or life-threatening illness
   6. qualification
   7. surgery

GRAPHIC ORGANIZER

Create a mind map to show your ideas about modern, traditional, and complimentary treatments and remedies. Include information about the treatments and when you would use them. Work with a partner. Compare your ideas.

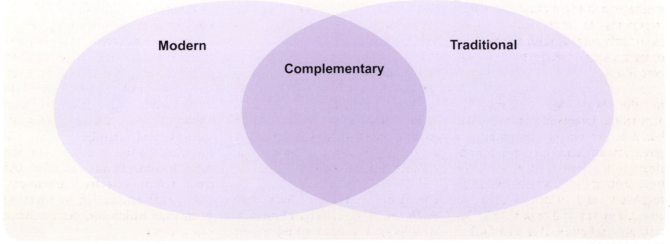

PRE-LISTENING QUESTIONS

1. Do you go to an alternative healer or a modern doctor? Why?
2. Do you prefer one system over the other? Why?

SITUATION: *Lara and Julie are discussing alternative treatments.*

Lara   I'd been going to the doctor for my headaches for years and he'd given me all sorts of tests and prescribed stronger and stronger painkillers. Then a friend gave me the name of an acupuncturist. I feel so much better now.

Julie   I can see that. I've heard that acupuncture can really help a lot of conditions.

Lara   Yes, from now on, I'm only using complementary medicine.

Julie   I understand why you would say that given your recent experience, but what about cases of serious diseases like cancer?

Lara   There are people who use alternatively therapies for cancer, too. Everyone has to make up their own mind, but I would definitely be open to trying some alternative treatments. A lot of them have been used for many years in other countries.

Julie   You're right to a point. But what if you get hit by a car? You're not going to sit around drinking herbal tea to cure yourself, are you?

Lara   No, of course not. I guess there are situations where you have no choice. But the point is, modern medicine actually creates a lot of complications because doctors don't take account of the whole person, their lifestyle etc.

Julie   I know exactly what you mean, but going the alternative route can be a real minefield. How can you tell the really professional practitioners from the charlatans? Look at all the alternative therapies out there – magnets, aromatherapy, massage, homeopathy…

Lara   Well, you do have to do a little research, but there are recognized bodies who give accreditation for a lot of alternative therapies.

Julie   And personal recommendations are pretty good too. Can I get a note of your acupuncturist's number? You know, just in case I ever need him.

CHECK FOR UNDERSTANDING

Are the following statements true or false?

1. Lara wasn't satisfied with the acupuncture treatment she received.
2. Julie agrees that Lara should never go back to a modern doctor.
3. Lara thinks that modern medicine is responsible for many health problems.
4. Julie thinks that you can trust most alternative healers.
5. Who do you agree with more, Julie or Lara?

Work with a partner. Compare your answers.

Quick Fact
In Africa, it is estimated that up to 80% of the population uses traditional medicine for primary health care.
- WHO

PRACTICE AND DISCUSSION

PERSONALIZATION

Complete these sentences with your own ideas.

> *Acupuncture can/cannot really help things like...*
>
> *People who avoid spending time in hospitals at all costs are...*
>
> *It's ... for a baby to be born at home.*
>
> *Using alternative medical treatments can...*
>
> *I just don't know enough about...*

Now share your sentences with a classmate.

DISCUSSION STRATEGIES - Agreeing

In order to keep a discussion going, and as a way of introducing new points, you need to show that you agree with the other speaker (even if you want to disagree later by adding but, however, nevertheless, etc.). Here are some ways of expressing agreement.

I can see/understand that.	**I understand/know why...**
You're right.	**That's true/right.**
I agree/go along with...	**You have a good point.**
I know/see what you mean.	**I'm with you.**
I think so.	**I couldn't agree more.**

Think of more examples.

Discussion Strategy in Action

Listen to the conversations. How do the speakers express agreement in each one?

Conversation   Expression

   1. _____

   2. _____

   3. _____

Discussion Practice

Work with a partner. Reply to these statements by agreeing. If you want to show a differing point of view, follow up with: but, however, or nevertheless. Continue the dialog.

1. Using alternative therapies such as acupuncture is a much gentler way of healing someone.
2. Conventional doctors take no notice of your lifestyle, diet, or psychological condition.
3. If I was in a traffic accident, the last person I would go to is a doctor who used some of these new, alternative treatments.
4. The problem with modern medicine is that there is so little focus on prevention.
5. Home births can be risky if there are complications.
6. You can't trust all alternative therapists.
7. There's not enough attention paid to the link between mind and body.
8. I think that acupuncture can really help with depression.

FURTHER ACTIVITIES

ROLE PLAY

> **Brainstorming:**
> How much input do you have in the treatment you get?
> Does your doctor/therapist actually listen to you when you talk about your symptoms?
> How much responsibility do you take for your own well-being?

Work with a partner and choose one of the following situations:
- A hypochondriac trying to talk to a very busy doctor
- A person with a strange illness trying to talk to a doctor who won't listen
- A person going to an alternative healer, but not sure about the treatments that are being suggested.
- A person with a mild problem going to a doctor, but not agreeing with the radical treatment that doctor is suggesting.
- A person with severe allergies going to an acupuncturist. The problem is the person is terrified of needles.

Consider the following:
- What are the symptoms and how do they affect the patient?
- How is the patient feeling physically and how does this affect his/her emotions and attitude towards the doctor?
- What does the doctor say and do to convince the patient this is the most effective treatment?
- What are the financial implications of the treatment for you and the patient?

Use the discussion strategies and other appropriate expressions, tone, emphasis, and body language.

ACTIVITY

Look at the treatments below. Which would you prefer to use, for example, to relieve a headache? Discuss these and other treatment options with your partner.

  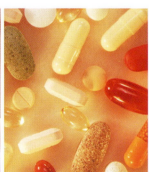 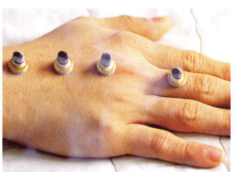

SPEECHES - A presentation on health treatments

Choose one of the forms of treatment below. Give a presentation to persuade potential patients that this would be the best treatment for them.

- Conventional drug treatments
- Massage
- Herbal remedies

- Acupuncture
- Yoga
- Aromatherapy

- Reiki healing
- Dietician
- Healing magnets

Consider:

What would attract clients to this particular form of treatment?
How long it will be effective.
How long they will have to continue the treatment.

How safe it is.
How expensive it is.
Any side-effects.

CONSOLIDATION AND RECYCLING

BUILDING VOCABULARY

What is your immediate emotional reaction to each treatment or therapy in the table? Describe your reaction using the words or phrases below or some of your own.

a rip off	effective	painful	traumatic
a waste of time	excellent	painless	unbalanced
addictive	fantastic	pleasant	uncomfortable
agony	foolish	relaxing	unhealthy
bad	good	safe	unhelpful
balanced	healthy	scientific	unpleasant
comfortable	helpful	side effects	unsafe
dangerous	no side effects	stupid	unscientific
disgusting	okay	terrible	useless

Treatments and therapies			
acupuncture		aromatherapy	
herbal remedies		inoculations	
yoga		drugs	
healing magnets		massage	
spiritual healing		crystals	

WRITING

Look at the list of treatments in the Speeches section on page 46. Choose one that you have had personal experience of or that you know something about. Write two or three paragraphs presenting a persuasive argument about why this is the best form of therapy.

Consider the following things:

- What does this treatment entail?
- What are the types of things it can be used to help?
- How safe is it?
- Are there any side effects?
- What are the advantages of this treatment over the others?
- Do you have any personal or anecdotal experiences?
- How highly would you recommend this?
- Are there any situations where you wouldn't recommend this?

REFLECTION

Do you think that it's useful to classify approaches to treatment in the following ways? What do they mean to you?

1. Western/Conventional vs. Traditional Chinese/Eastern
2. Conventional vs. Alternative/Complementary Therapies
3. Interventionist vs. Natural
4. Mechanical vs. Holistic (mind-body balance)

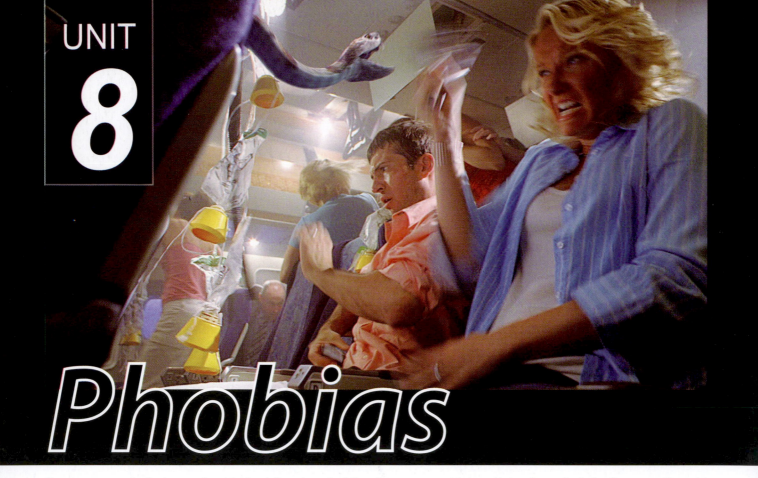

Phobias

For many people their vacation starts at the airport while others are sent into a state of paralysis by the mere thought of flying. This week we explore phobias with Dr. Todd Steven, author of several books on the subject.

As the years go by, I'm getting more nervous about air travel. Is that a common phobia?

Lots of people are nervous about flying but have no problem getting on a plane to go on vacation. They don't have a phobia. The word 'phobia' may come from the Greek word for fear, but a phobia is a strong, unreasonable fear or hatred of something. It is persistent, irrational, and intense, and it usually leads to avoidance and panic. It is a relatively common type of anxiety disorder and yes, fear of flying, known as aviophobia, is pretty common.

How do you treat something that is irrational?

Phobias can be treated with exposure and fear reduction techniques. Basically, we gradually expose the patient to their fear until they become less sensitive to it. We often do that along with counseling so that they understand their own thought patterns and reactions. In many cases, anti-anxiety or anti-depressant medication can also be helpful, especially during the early stages of therapy.

How do you apply those techniques to aviophobia?

These techniques help people to associate flying with more comfortable feelings, but education is also useful. Once people understand how aircraft fly and other aspects of aviation, they can overcome their fear. However, fear of flying is actually very complex because there are many different factors and other phobias at play. Often people are concerned about flying over water, or flying at night, they may fear turbulence or worry about being hijacked, some may have a fear of heights while others fear crowds, they may be concerned that they will have a panic attack in a place where escape (the natural reaction to fear) would be difficult. Some are afraid because they are not in control and it is common for women to become more afraid of flying once they have a child. An earlier traumatic flight can also trigger a fear of flying. So before we start treatment, we must understand the individual's concerns.

That must be why aviophobia gets so much attention.

Possibly. Fear of flying also receives more attention than many other phobias because air travel is difficult for people to avoid and because it may prevent a person from going on vacation or visiting family and friends, and it can harm someone's career if their job involves a lot of air travel. The media are also a factor. Airplane crashes get more attention than they really deserve because of the high casualty rate even though the overall safety record of air travel is very good and continues to improve. In fact, the most dangerous part of a flight is the drive to the airport.

VOCABULARY

Here are some words that will be useful in this unit. How many do you know? Work with a partner to figure out the meaning of any words that you don't know.

anxious	fear	situation
condition	panic attack	terror
crowds	phobia	therapy
dominate	physical	trapped
environment	irrational	uncomfortable

What other words and phrases do you know related to the topic?

VOCABULARY ACTIVITIES

A. Read the paragraph and circle the words that are not used correctly. Replace the incorrect words with words from the list above. Remember to use the correct word form.

> People who are terror in situations where they are surrounded by lots of people, sometimes become very scared, their hearts start to race and they develop a therapy. Sometimes they may struggle to breathe or start to sweat a lot. This physical be extremely fear. It can distress someone's life so much that they can't carry on a normal lifestyle. The fears are often rational but they feel very real to the person suffering from them. Some types of anger can help with the problems but it often takes a lot of work to get over a phobia.

Work with a partner. Compare your answers.

B. Write the correct form of a word from the list above next to its description.

1. It doesn't make sense and there's no real logic in it but it is the way you feel.
2. You are very afraid of something in particular and this fear can affect the way you act.
3. You start to feel very nervous and your breath starts to come quickly. Sometimes your heart will start racing and you become very distressed.
4. There are lots of people all around. It is difficult to get away from them.
5. The doctor or healer can try to help you by talking to you or giving you drugs, physical manipulations, or cures.
6. You are in a closed situation or space and you cannot escape.

GRAPHIC ORGANIZER

Add at least three examples for each type of phobia. Work with a partner. Compare your ideas.

DIFFERENT PHOBIAS

ANIMAL	NATURAL ENVIRONMENT	MEDICAL	PHYSICAL SITUATION
_____	_____	_____	_____
_____	_____	_____	_____
_____	_____	_____	_____
_____	_____	_____	_____

POINTS OF VIEW *You can get over a phobia.*

PRE-LISTENING QUESTIONS

1. What are the symptoms of a phobia?
2. Do you think that people sometimes exaggerate their fears?

SITUATION: *Isadora and Lee are discussing Isadora's fears.*

Isadora	I just got a great new job, but I'll be working on the 45th floor.
Lee	What's wrong with that? The views must be great.
Isadora	I'm acrophobic. I can't bear to be near the windows. Plus I'm claustrophobic so I can't get into an elevator.
Lee	I forgot about all your phobias. Did you tell them about your phobias in the interview?
Isadora	Yes, they said they would help me, but I'm still worried that I'll look foolish; not everyone is as understanding as you.

Lee	I know what it's like. I used to have arachnophobia. I couldn't go into a room if I even thought there was a spider in there.
Isadora	How did you overcome that?
Lee	Well, I know people who have successfully used hypnotherapy, but I wasn't too sure about that so I had exposure therapy. I was gradually introduced to more frightening experiences until I was no longer afraid. So it started with just being close to a spider then holding a fake spider, then a real one then holding bigger and bigger spiders. Perhaps we could do something similar to help you. Why don't we practice going up in an elevator, just one floor at a time so you're not in it for too long each time? And we can get closer to windows at each level too to help you get over both phobias.
Isadora	No, you don't understand. I get terrible panic attacks.
Lee	Well, we can develop techniques for relaxing and relieving those. You have to believe in yourself, you can't let this dominate your life. You don't want to lose this job, do you?
Isadora	No, you're right. I know it's irrational and it's about time I faced my fears.

CHECK FOR UNDERSTANDING

1. What are Isadora's two main fears?
2. What might her fears jeopardize?
3. What does Lee suggest that she do?
4. Do you think his ideas will help Isadora?
5. Why is Lee sympathetic?

Work with a partner. Compare your answers.

Quick Fact

In 2007, researchers at the University of New South Wales, Australia developed nasal sprays to deliver compounds which may help people overcome phobias.

PRACTICE AND DISCUSSION

PERSONALIZATION

Complete these sentences with your own ideas.

Isadora should...

Isadora is being...

The best way to overcome a fear of...

I have a fear of...

I know someone who is afraid of...

Their fear of ... started when...

Now share your sentences with a classmate.

DISCUSSION STRATEGIES - Convincing and suggesting

We use different expressions and grammatical forms when trying to convince people to do something they don't necessarily want to do. Look at these expressions. Can you think of any others?

You have to...	**I do understand but...**
Look at the facts...	**That's what you should...**
If you don't..., it will...	**I'm sure you can manage to...**
It will be easier if...	**All you have to do is...**

Think of more examples.

Discussion Strategy in Action

Listen to the conversations. For each one, write down the expression used to convince the other person to do something. Was it effective?

Conversation	Expression	Effective?
1	_____ _____	Y ☐ N ☐
2	_____ _____	Y ☐ N ☐
3	_____ _____	Y ☐ N ☐
4	_____ _____	Y ☐ N ☐

Discussion Practice

Work with a partner. Take turns trying to convince your partner to do these things:

1. Go somewhere they're afraid of going.
2. Touch something they don't want to touch.
3. Go near things that make them scared.
4. Eat something they wouldn't normally try.

FURTHER ACTIVITIES

ROLE PLAY

Brainstorming:

Think about the kind of situations in which phobias can create difficulties.

How would the person with the phobia try to avoid doing something?

How can you convince someone who has phobia to overcome it?

Work with a partner. For each of the following situations, take turns convincing your partner to do something they don't want to do.

Phobia	Situation
fear of heights	You are on a long hike and have to cross a bridge over a very deep canyon in order to finish the walk. It is not possible to go back.
fear of closed spaces	You are late for an important meeting that you are going to with a colleague and there are traffic jams everywhere. The only fast way to get there is to take the subway which is very crowded.
fear of hospitals	A close friend has been injured in a car crash and is now in the hospital. You know that you should visit him/her but you are so afraid of hospitals that it's really difficult.
fear of public speaking	You are afraid of public speaking but your boss has said that if you can't make a speech at the next sales conference, you won't be promoted.

ACTIVITY

Answer this questionnaire. Work with a partner. Compare your answers.

	Agree	Not sure	Disagree
1. Most phobias can be related to a traumatic experience, possibly at a young age.			
2. Some people with phobias like the attention they get from others.			
3. Most phobias are not very serious.			
4. If people really want to, they can get over their phobias.			
5. Phobias often relate to real dangers.			
6. You should not make light of phobias, they are always very serious.			

SPEECHES - It's safe to fly

Imagine that you are helping people overcome their fear of flying. You need to give reasons why it is safe to fly and offer several suggestions for ways the people can get over their fears.

Consider the following:

- What might make someone worried/nervous?
- What are the real or imagined reasons for their fears?
- What kind of facts might reassure them?
- What kind of steps can they take to help themselves feel more relaxed and confident?
- Use appropriate language to convince them that they will be okay.

Give your talk to a group of students who will pretend to be afraid of flying. Hold a question and answer session at the end.

CONSOLIDATION AND RECYCLING

BUILDING VOCABULARY

Look at these word roots. They can be put together to make another word.
Complete the chart with the combined word and its definition.

			word	meaning
photo (light)	graphy (to write)	=	_____	_____
phone (sound, speak)	tele (far off)	=	_____	_____
arachna (spider)	phobia (fear)	=	_____	_____
biblion (books)	graphy (to write)	=	_____	_____
cracy (type of government)	demos (people)	=	_____	_____
claustro (enclosed space)	phobia (fear)	=	_____	_____
ology (study)	psycho (the mind)	=	_____	_____
acro (air/heights)	phobia (fear)	=	_____	_____

Work with a partner. Add examples of other words with similar roots.

WRITING

Choose one of these letters and write a response giving advice on what they can do to help cope with their phobia.

1. I have a very strange phobia and I don't know what I can do about it. I am terrified of anything that flutters – moths, butterflies, and even birds. This only affects me when I'm inside. When I'm outside, I'm perfectly fine. And I don't mind other insects; I just get in a panic whenever fluttery things come inside. Luckily, it doesn't come up too often, but it is a bit embarrassing.

2. I suffer from a phobia which is making my social life very difficult. I can't eat in front of other people. I don't know what it's caused by – I certainly do like eating. Whenever I'm with other people the thought of eating in front of them makes me feel sick and my throat closes. I get very stressed about it. I usually avoid situations by making excuses like not being hungry or having some sort of stomach upset. But people are beginning to think that I'm rude when they invite me for dinner and I don't eat. At the same time, I don't want to be left out.

3. I'm not sure where this fear of the dark came from. I can't sleep with the lights out. If by accident, someone turns out the lights, I get almost paralyzed. I just can't move – I seem to lose control of my limbs and my heart starts beating like crazy. It seems ridiculous. I'm a grown man and I shouldn't have this sort of problem. I also do not dare go to night clubs or in the subway for fear of the dark.

REFLECTION

1. Has this unit informed you about any phobias that you didn't know about before?
2. Has it changed your attitude towards phobias? If so, how?
3. What do you think is the best way of dealing with people who have phobias?

Life's Luxuries

When you pick up a magazine these days, it seems that more than half of the pages are taken up by glossy ads for luxury items. Even the articles in many magazines are like ads, encouraging readers to live beyond their means, chasing a dream that they could be happier if they ate at the best restaurants, drove a certain car, or redecorated their home in the latest style. Features on designer clothes and accessories, expensive cosmetics, spas, and exotic vacations fill many pages even in developing countries where many may aspire to have such things, but only a small minority of the population can actually afford them.

In a world filled with so much poverty it can be hard to justify such excesses, but what some consider an extravagance is a necessity to others.

The modern work environment has changed many people's lifestyles beyond recognition. In some jobs, particularly in sales and finance, there is now an expectation that you will dress in a particular way and keep up a certain level of grooming as an outward demonstration of your success. This creates pressure, particularly on young people starting out in their new career. It is not always clear whether this pressure is real or imagined. Would someone's job really be in jeopardy if they didn't choose a glamorous designer suit or if they went to work by bus instead of driving an expensive sports car? It is unlikely. However, there is a perceived requirement in certain jobs and social positions to keep up or set ever higher standards in order to impress others.

There are other pressures too. Because of the long hours and more sedentary style of modern work, people need to find new ways of relieving stress and keeping healthy. This might help them justify their membership of a glamorous gym or spa that they feel is an indispensable part of their lives.

Meanwhile, people on a lower pay scale remain mystified that anyone could pay what for them may be a week's wage for something as mundane as a pedicure.

In many societies, having domestic help at home is the norm while in other societies it can be viewed as the ultimate extravagance and even a sign of laziness. With increasing numbers of families where both parents work, it is often impossible to function without someone to help with the children, the housekeeping, or the gardening. Domestic help provides these people with what has become one of the greatest luxuries of modern life – time.

When the gap between the rich and the poor can be so divisive, there is a need to balance the natural desire to reward oneself with the best that you can afford with the needs of others, but don't we all need a special luxury to enjoy from time to time, whether it takes the form of a CD from a street market or a diamond ring?

VOCABULARY

Here are some words that will be useful in this unit. How many do you know? Work with a partner to figure out the meaning of any words that you don't know.

charming	famous	lavish	ostentatious
crave	glamorous	luxurious	status symbol
exotic	heir / heiress	mundane	wealthy
extravagant	highly paid	opulent	weird

What other words and phrases do you know related to the topic?

VOCABULARY ACTIVITIES

A. Find a word from about to complete the list of synonyms. Then find a synonym for each of the remaining words in the list above.

1. well off, rich, _____
2. extravagant, expensive, _____
3. celebrated, well known, _____
4. interesting, fascinating, _____
5. iconic, representative, _____

B. Make a list of items, people, and places that could be accurately described using the vocabulary above. Work with a partner. Compare your ideas.

DESCRIPTION	ITEMS	PEOPLE	PLACES
_____	_____	_____	_____
_____	_____	_____	_____
_____	_____	_____	_____
_____	_____	_____	_____
_____	_____	_____	_____

GRAPHIC ORGANIZER

List examples of luxuries for the following categories. Work with a partner. Compare your ideas.

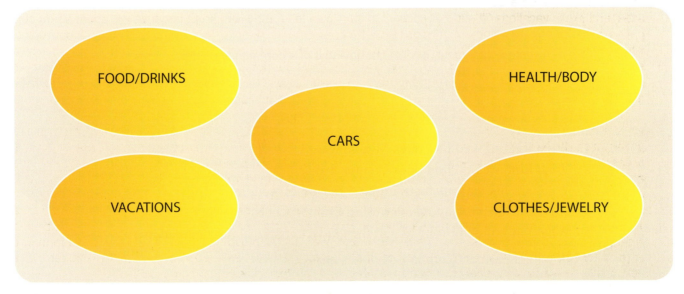

FOOD/DRINKS
HEALTH/BODY
CARS
VACATIONS
CLOTHES/JEWELRY

PRE-LISTENING QUESTIONS

1. How much would you spend on your wedding?
2. Is it okay for people to show off their wealth at a big wedding or other event?

SITUATION: *Connor and Minnie are discussing their wedding plans.*

Minnie	Did you have a look at the wedding brochures I left out?
Connor	The what?
Minnie	These wedding brochures. I'd left them on the table by the stairs. I've marked the pages of the best packages.
Connor	I'm sorry I didn't notice them.
Minnie	I doesn't matter, we can look at them now. What do you think of this one?
Connor	I'm not sure. I mean, it looks kind of expensive.
Minnie	Don't worry, they offer financing and my parents have saved up some money.
Connor	I'm not really sure about a big wedding, are you?
Minnie	Look at the way they've decorated the room in this picture. It looks fantastic.
Connor	I don't think it's right to have a big, luxurious wedding. Can we or our families really afford it? We're going to have a big mortgage to pay off as it is.
Minnie	What's that got to do with it? In my family we always have big weddings. My parents would be embarrassed if we had a small one. I'm not asking for a million-dollar wedding, but it's my day and I want it to be very special.
Connor	I'm not saying it won't be special. It can just be simple, intimate, can't it? Why don't we just rent a room in the community center and have a light buffet?
Minnie	Well, I've made an appointment with a wedding planner who will go through all the possible options.
Connor	I think that we should set out a budget before going any further. You don't want us to start life together with financial difficulties, do you?
Minnie	What are you, an accountant? Don't you get it? This is my wedding we're talking about.
Connor	It's my wedding too and I don't want to start our life together bankrupt because we spent so much on a fancy ceremony.
Minnie	Okay, I'll scale it back a bit, but I'm not having it at a community center.

CHECK FOR UNDERSTANDING

1. What kind of wedding does Minnie want?
2. What kind of wedding does Connor want?
3. What are his reasons for wanting this type of wedding?
4. How does Minnie avoid answering Connor's questions?
5. What kind of compromise will they have to make about the wedding?

Work with a partner. Compare your answers.

Quick Fact
The Diamond Wedding Gown, probably the world's most expensive wedding dress, has 150 carats of diamonds and was valued at $12 million in 2007.

PRACTICE AND DISCUSSION

PERSONALIZATION

Complete these sentences with your own ideas.

I agree with Minnie/Connor because…

Big weddings can be a problem because…

Getting into a lot of debt for something you don't absolutely need is…

The best kind of luxury is…

Now share your sentences with a classmate.

DISCUSSION STRATEGIES - Avoiding answering questions

For various reasons, we might want to avoid answering direct questions when in a discussion. Here are some ways of doing this:

- by changing the topic or redirecting the discussion
- by using the following expressions:

I'm sorry I don't remember…	**I'm not sure…**
I couldn't say…	**I can't answer that, but…**
I don't know what you mean…	**What's that got to do with it?**
I'll give that some thought…	**I'm not interested in going into that…**
Let's not talk about/go into that now.	**There are more important things…**

Think of more examples.

Discussion Strategy in Action

Listen to the conversations. For each one, note how the person avoids answering the question directly.

1. _____
2. _____
3. _____
4. _____

Discussion Practice

Work with a partner. How do you feel about the following items? Are they luxuries? Discuss each item. Use the discussion strategies above to avoid answering any questions your partner asks about each item.

1. an expensive holiday
2. the latest mobile phone
3. a rare painting
4. a video camera
5. membership at an exclusive club
6. a new computer
7. a meal in a nice restaurant
8. a luxury sports car
9. an MP3 player
10. concert tickets

FURTHER ACTIVITIES

ROLE PLAY

> **Brainstorming:**
>
> Think of the kinds of status symbols that are important to people. Why are some things craved more than others? How important is design and image?

Work with a partner. Take turns to play the role of a journalist and a famous person in the following situations.

The magazine journalist interviews people known for their luxurious lifestyles. They need to give interviews, but are usually unwilling to give any more information than necessary, though.

Consider the following:
- What would be of interest and make a fun article?
- How can the journalist lead the famous person to give the information?
- What kinds of questions would catch the interviewee off guard?
- Think about what the famous person's lifestyle must be like.
- The famous person wants to give a positive impression, but doesn't want people to know too much about their financial situation or their personal life. How will they be able to gracefully deflect direct questions and still look good?

The movie star	You are a highly paid movie star who has had a series of bad films and a bad marriage. You are known for your lavish lifestyle, parties, and expensive cars – and you have drawn a lot of criticism for this. However, you are trying to relaunch your image and your career. You don't want people to know the details of your expensive divorce.
The business	You are a young and attractive owner of an upcoming chain of clothing boutiques. You come from a humble background. You work hard and play hard. You are known as a jetsetter and collector of extravagant jewelry, however, at the moment you are going through serious financial difficulties. You don't want people to know this for business and personal reasons.
The heir/heiress	You are heir/heiress to a huge business fortune and are trying to make it as a pop singer. No one will take you seriously because they think that you are spoilt and have every luxury you can imagine. You are determined to downplay that image, but at the same time it's difficult to hide the fact that everything you wear or use is the latest in fashion and design.

ACTIVITY

Work with a partner. Imagine you are stuck on a desert island. Which five luxuries would you want to have with you? Consider the following:
- What you could enjoy over and over.
- What you wouldn't get tired of or bored with.
- What wouldn't break down on a desert island.
- What would make you feel happy.

Discuss your choices.

SPEECHES - A radio commercial

Write a radio advertisement for a luxury item. Then present your ad to the class.
Consider the following:
- Who are you aiming the commercial at?
- What would appeal to your potential customers?
- What would convince them to buy the product?
- What kind of approach would you take to the commercial – a direct or indirect selling approach?
- What sorts of things would enhance the commercial? Music? Sound effects? Celebrity presenters?

BUILDING VOCABULARY

Look at these items and make a list of adjectives for each one. Include comparative and superlative forms.

_____   _____   _____
_____   _____   _____
_____   _____   _____

_____   _____   _____
_____   _____   _____
_____   _____   _____

_____   _____   _____
_____   _____   _____
_____   _____   _____

WRITING

Choose one luxury product and write an advertising brochure for it. Consider the following:

- The style of the brochure and what kind of message you want to get across.
- The type of language you need to use.
- Any symbols, images, or celebrities you might need to help get the message across.
- The market sector you want to target.
- If you want to include any particular sale or promotion in the brochure.

REFLECTION

1. What kind of luxury products are the most popular in your country with your age group?
2. How has the attitude towards luxury changed in your country in the last few years?
3. What is one 'luxury' that you allow yourself everyday?

Good Service

When is customer service really customer disservice?

People are increasingly dissatisfied with the level of service they receive. Here, we take a look at some of the things that people most frequently complain about.

Rude servers

Everyone has a story about a rude or incompetent server in a bar or restaurant. Poor service can really spoil a special meal or important business meeting. In countries like the U.S.A., tips make up a significant part of a server's wage so they have a clear incentive to treat the customer well. However, some servers become aggressive when they do not receive what they think is a fair tip.

Being put on hold

Companies are very willing to talk to you when making a sale, but as soon as you have a problem or you need more information, you find it impossible to speak to someone who can help you. All too often, you are put on hold and forced to listen to a recorded message assuring you, "Your call is important to us" or you are subjected to endlessly repeated music, lists of options to choose from, and then more recorded messages. If you ever manage to actually talk to a human being, they usually quickly say that it is not their department and they put you on hold again.

Help lines

Many products such as computers are sold with access to a help line which is supposed to offer support to the consumer. Unfortunately, many of the people working on the help lines are not helpful at all. They are not really qualified for the job, they don't listen to the problem, and they often don't offer any workable solutions. Sometimes they simply read from a script. To add insult to injury, often callers are charged a higher rate for these telephone calls.

Overcharging by trades people

We are dependent on electricians, plumbers, mechanics, and builders to help us. If you do not have a good relationship with reliable trades people, you can really be at their mercy. Complaints include exorbitant prices, unprofessional work, and sometimes, never even finishing the job. If you have water running all over your floor or your car is broken down in the middle of a snow storm, you are not usually in a position to negotiate a fair price and people are often taken advantage of by 'cowboy' companies or individuals. Many women feel that they are particularly vulnerable.

Taxi drivers who take longer routes, understaffing at airport check-in desks, anything to do with civil servants, the list goes on and on. So what can we do about it? Most people simply do not have the time, energy, or inclination to follow up when things go wrong, but if we did complain more whenever things go wrong perhaps, attitudes would change.

VOCABULARY

Here are some words that will be useful in this unit. How many do you know? Work with a partner to figure out the meaning of any words that you don't know.

after-sales service	consumer rights	put on hold	support
call center	get through to	put through to	take responsibility
compensate	initiative	refund	talk from a script
complimentary	policy	rip off	tip

What other words and phrases do you know related to the topic?

VOCABULARY ACTIVITIES

A. Fill in the blanks with words or phrases from the list above. Remember to use the correct word forms.

There are increasing numbers of 1. _____ where the employees have to deal with inquiries about a number of different products and services they know little about. Often, when consumers try to get help they get 2. _____ and have to listen to a repeated recorded message or monotonous music. They are then 3. _____ someone who is not really interested and do not get the level of 4. _____ that they require or deserve.

Many workers in call centers are badly paid and are not given much 5. _____ for improving their service. They are bored. Many call center workers just end up 6. _____ and are not permitted to use their 7. _____ when it comes to actually helping the consumer. In addition, they are basically anonymous and have no real relationship with the person on the other end of the phone. It's difficult for consumers to demand their 8. _____ or get a 9._____ when they can't 10. _____ anyone who will help them.

B. Read these quotes. What is happening?
1. I'm sorry. You were slow and the food was cold. I'm only leaving you five percent.
2. I have been listening to this horrible music for 20 minutes. No one seems to be answering.
3. I'm so sorry that your CD player didn't work properly. We don't have anymore in stock so I'll put a credit on your card.
4. I don't want to speak to the sales department, I need technical help. You're the fifth person I've talked to so far.
5. We paid for a luxury cruise and found ourselves on a rusty little boat that made us seasick.

GRAPHIC ORGANIZER

List ten things about customer services that annoy you. Work with a partner. Compare your ideas.

MOST ANNOYING

1. _____
2. _____
3. _____
4. _____
5. _____
6. _____
7. _____
8. _____
9. _____
10. _____

LESS ANNOYING

PRE-LISTENING QUESTIONS

1. Have you ever been in a situation where you were really unhappy about something you bought? What did you do?
2. How forceful should you be when you are complaining?

SITUATION: *Ethan is discussing his complaints with the hotel's front desk clerk.*

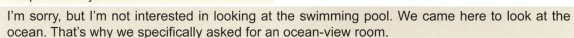

Ethan	I don't like to complain, but we are very unhappy.
FDC	Oh, I am sorry to hear that, Sir. How can I help?
Ethan	The main problem is that the room is nothing like the one shown in the brochure. We booked a luxury room and we've found ourselves in tiny box with no view. Plus, the standard of cleanliness is poor and the service so far has been appalling.
FDC	I'm not sure I understand. It's a perfectly adequate room. The rooms can't all be identical to the brochure and you can see the pool from your room.
Ethan	I'm sorry, but I'm not interested in looking at the swimming pool. We came here to look at the ocean. That's why we specifically asked for an ocean-view room.
FDC	You must understand that it's impossible to have everyone in a room that looks out on the ocean. The building is just not designed that way.
Ethan	If that's the case, you should state it clearly in your brochure.
FDC	Well, I'll have to look into that.
Ethan	I think that you should do something to compensate us for all of this.
FDC	Compensate you? You've been here for two days already. Why didn't you tell me immediately?
Ethan	You're right, I probably should have done, but I was tired when we arrived and I didn't want to upset my wife. I think that the least you can do is give us some money back.
FDC	That's just not possible.
Ethan	You can't expect us to pay these high charges for this poor level of accommodation. It's just not satisfactory. If you can't help then I'd like to speak with someone who can. I'd like to see the manager, please.
FDC	I'm very sorry that you're not happy. Normally our hotel has a no refund policy, but I'll discuss this with the manager. In the mean time, I'd like to offer you a complimentary meal in our restaurant tonight and I'll see if we have an ocean-view room available.

CHECK FOR UNDERSTANDING

1. What are Ethan's main complaints about the room?
2. What are the front desk clerk's excuses?
3. What kind of threat does Ethan have to use before he gets any action?
4. Describe Ethan's manner when he is complaining.
5. Were Ethan's complaints justified?

Work with a partner. Compare your answers.

Quick Fact
A 75-year-old woman in the U.S.A. was fined $345 for damaging a phone company receptionist's monitor, keyboard, and phone with a hammer because she was frustrated by the company's poor customer service.

PRACTICE AND DISCUSSION

PERSONALIZATION

Complete these sentences with your own ideas.

In Ethan's place, I would…

When I complain, I…

If someone complains to me, I…

The last time I complained about something…

I wouldn't bother complaining about…

Now share your sentences with a classmate.

DISCUSSION STRATEGIES - Complaining

There are a number of ways we can make complaints. Work with a partner. Consider which of these you would use to make strong complaints.

I don't like to complain but…	The problem is that…
That's not really the issue…	We are very disappointed.
I have to disagree with you.	The least you can do is…
You can't expect…	I have the right…
I don't care if…	That's not good enough.
If you can't …, I will…	I insist…
I want to speak to …, immediately.	I am unhappy with…

Think of more examples.

Discussion Strategy in Action

Listen to the conversations. Decide if the person's complaint/request is mild or strong. Summarize what is being discussed.

Conversation	Strong	Mild	Topic
1			
2			
3			
4			
5			

Discussion Practice

Work with a partner. Take turns making complaints in these situations.

1. You recently bought a computer. It isn't working. You don't know much about computers.
2. You bought a new coat last week in a special sale. The seam on a sleeve has come apart.
3. You just got your car repaired, but it still does not run very well. The mechanics are not very helpful.
4. The person who is serving you has been rude and ignores you. It is a very nice restaurant and you are taking your friend out for his/her birthday.

FURTHER ACTIVITIES

ROLE PLAY

> **Brainstorming:**
>
> Think of difficult situations when you need to complain about something. What are effective and ineffective ways of complaining? Does it ever help to lose your temper?

Work with a partner. For each situation below, one of you must complain to the other. Be as diplomatic as possible, but get your point across. Take turns playing the role of the person complaining. Continue each dialog until you have settled the complaint fairly.

1. The customer ordered 24 items from a supplier but only 8 arrived. The supplier insists that they sent 24. They use another company to make the deliveries.

2. The customer went to see a movie but had a terrible time because some of the other people in the movie theater were very loud and rude. The customer wants a refund. The manager thinks that it is not his/her fault if members of the public are inconsiderate.

3. A week ago your partner's friend installed your car radio. He charged you much less than normal, but now the radio does not work and he won't fix it.

4. A family had a big party at an expensive hotel. Unfortunately, a fight broke out causing a considerable amount of damage. The manager of the hotel wants compensation from the head of the family.

ACTIVITY

Make a list of examples of poor customer service. Work with a partner. Compare your lists then discuss reasons why good customer service is important and can benefit the company. Suggest ways of improving customer service in different types of companies.

SPEECHES - Know your consumer rights

How important is it to know and exercise your rights as a consumer? Give a short speech about this. Consider the following:

- What are your rights as a consumer? Do you have fewer rights if the item or service is inexpensive?
- What are your responsibilities as a consumer?
- Why is it good for everyone if people complain when service is bad? What happens if people don't complain?
- What are the right and the wrong ways to complain?
- How can you be sure that your complaints are effective?
- Use examples from your own experience where you complained effectively or where you could have complained more effectively.

Give your speech to a small group. Hold a short question and answer session afterwards.

BUILDING VOCABULARY

Replace the underlined words with a phrasal verb from the list below. Remember to use the correct word form.

back up	break down	fix up
get through	pay back	rip off
show up	wipe off	wipe out

I tried to <u>connect on the phone</u> to the electronics company because my new TV <u>has stopped working</u>. I wanted someone to come and repair it. When I finally spoke to a woman she said that they couldn't find any record of my purchase because a computer virus had <u>erased</u> all their files and they hadn't <u>saved</u> the files. She couldn't do anything. I said that it was a complete <u>swindle</u> and I wanted her to <u>refund</u> the full price of the TV immediately. Suddenly her attitude changed and she promised that a repair man would <u>appear</u> the next day.

WRITING

Write a letter or email of complaint. Consider the following:

- What the situation is and what you want to achieve by complaining.
- Who would be the best person to complain to?
- How to clearly set out the situation and effectively get what you want in the end (think about the tone of your letter etc.).
- What your consumer rights are in this situation.
- What course of action you can/will take if you do not get a satisfactory response.

Compare your completed letter/email with your classmates' letters. Which do you think are most/least effective? Why?

REFLECTION

1. What approach do you think you will take when complaining in the future?
2. What are some of the difficulties when complaining in a different country? What are ways of overcoming these?
3. Is the customer always right?

UNIT 11

Fans

Anyone who consistently impresses us with their talents is worthy of adulation. Sporting achievement is perhaps the perfect vehicle for creating wholesome heroes and loyal fans will go to great lengths to see every game and collect all kinds of memorabilia associated with their team or favorite athlete.

The entertainment industry has probably produced an even wider fan base than sports. The best actors, singers, musicians, and dancers attract thousands of fans. Talent is important, but it also helps if they are good looking. But even fictional characters from a book or movie can have a loyal following. Characters such as Harry Potter draw fans from all ages and many cultures.

People can now become famous, or at least infamous, for doing very little and these 'minor celebrities' also have fans that follow every aspect of their lives: the parties they go to, the people they date and the trouble they get into.

Following the actions of an individual or group of famous people can be a useful way of bonding with family, friends, and strangers. Fan clubs can be established to share the fans' common interests and many stars assist their better organized fan clubs and may interact with their fans through Internet chats and blogs.

Unfortunately, some celebrities can become so caught up in their own fame that they disrespect the people who actually put them in the limelight – the fans. When thrilled fans finally meet their idols, it can be very disappointing to find that someone they have hero-worshipped for so long can be so rude and self-centered in person. On the other hand, fans can also be fickle and when they start to find the object of their adoration less interesting, the fans quickly disappear from view and the celebrity's 'fifteen minutes of fame' is suddenly up.

Most people would admit that they admire a certain celebrity, sports team, or athlete. Some people may also admit that they are such a devoted fan that they have seen every movie a director has made or they can recall the tiniest detail of their team's match data, but being such a devoted fan is something that people usually grow out of. They may still be interested in their team as they get older, but wouldn't be too upset if they can't get to every game any more.

However, some fans can become obsessive. Following their idol can take over the fan's life and there have been cases of extreme fans turning into stalkers. Sometimes the stalking consists of relatively harmless but annoying activities such as hanging around the house, leaving gifts, and even going through their idol's garbage. But it can also take on more dangerous turns as demonstrated by the case of the stalker who tried to kill President Reagan just to get Jodi Foster's attention.

VOCABULARY

Here are some words that will be useful in this unit. How many do you know? Work with a partner to figure out the meaning of any words that you don't know.

aggressive	**damage**	**idol**	**security**
anti-social behavior	**devastate**	**obsess**	**stalk**
ban	**fame**	**paparazzi**	**thrill**
celebrity	**fixation**	**provoke**	**worship**

What other words and phrases do you know related to the topic?

VOCABULARY ACTIVITIES

A. Complete the text with words from the list above. Remember to use the correct word form.

A lot of 1. _____ complain about being 2. _____ and harassed, but in reality, it happens to a lot of ordinary men and women every day. 3. _____ people, like film stars, are often 4. _____ when their photos are repeatedly taken by the 5. _____ or 6. _____ fans. They often have to take on extra 7. _____ to protect themselves from this. However, ordinary people can also have 8. _____ experiences when people develop a 9. _____ on them and follow them, send them unwelcome letters, emails and phone messages. This kind of 10. _____ can be very 11. _____ for the victim and often causes severe anxiety, depression, or other ailments. In some places the police do take it seriously and will 12. _____ the stalker from coming close to the victim. However, sometimes they don't and this can have very serious consequences as in the cases of John Lennon (who was murdered) and Monica Seles (who was injured during a tennis match).

B. Each group of words contains one word that does not belong there. Make a sentence with that word. Work with a partner. Compare your ideas.

1. famous	celebrated	collected
2. worship	idolize	ban
3. aggressive behavior	anti-social behavior	worshipful behavior
4. thrill	disappoint	devastate
5. obsession	fixation	paparazzi

GRAPHIC ORGANIZER

List words to describe a typical fan for each of these. Work with a partner. Compare your ideas.

Sports team	_____
Athlete	_____
Teenage pop group	_____
Classical singer	_____
Computer game	_____
Author	_____

PRE-LISTENING QUESTIONS

1. Think of situations where sports fans got out of control. What happened?
2. What do you think the authorities should do about this?

SITUATION: *Kim and Amy are discussing out of control fans.*

Kim	I can't believe it. Next week's concert has been cancelled. I've been looking forward to it for months.
Amy	That's too bad. Why was it cancelled?
Kim	There have been some problems recently with rival gangs that support other groups and a fight broke out at the last concert. A few people ended up in hospital and there was some damage to properties near the stadium. Now everyone is being punished because of a few stupid people.
Amy	That's so frustrating. Look, I know you were looking forward to the concert, but on the other hand, it's not acceptable for fans to behave like that, is it?
Kim	I know, but it was only a few people and those individuals should be punished, not everyone.
Amy	I had no idea music fans behaved like that. Maybe the authorities felt they had to take drastic action. And there will be other concerts.
Kim	You obviously don't understand what it's like. I'm really passionate about this group, I love listening to their music, discussing it with my friends, buying merchandise, planning for the concerts. A big part of my life revolves around supporting this group. I really feel like I'm part of something and now I feel devastated.
Amy	I do understand that. I mean, I'm not into music that much, but I'm a huge basketball fan.
Kim	Are you? I didn't know that.
Amy	Yes, I never miss a game. And I have a blog which I update with the stats from every game before the end of that day no matter where I am or what I'm doing. I can tell you the scores and highlights of every game for the last five years.
Kim	Okay, that pretty much makes you the most devoted sports fan I've met, and a little weird too. I can't believe I didn't know that about you.

Quick Fact
A fan that only supports a popular and successful team or athlete is called a fair-weather fan or a bandwagon fan.

✔ CHECK FOR UNDERSTANDING

1. What has happened to the concert Kim was supposed to go to? Why?
2. Why does Kim think this is unfair?
3. Why does Amy think that it's not unfair? What do you think?
4. Why does Kim feel "devastated"?
5. What did Kim learn about Amy?

Work with a partner. Compare your answers.

PRACTICE AND DISCUSSION

PERSONALIZATION

Complete these sentences with your own ideas.

> *Fans who are out of control should/shouldn't…*
> *Fans who are well-behaved should/shouldn't…*
> *It is/isn't the responsibility of the team to…*
> *Anti-social behavior such as … is…*
> *Real sports fans enjoy…*

Now share your sentences with a classmate.

DISCUSSION STRATEGIES - Acknowledging anger and emotions

That's really too bad.

I really sympathize/feel for you.

That's so true.

You must be…

That must have been…

I do understand…

Think of more examples.

Discussion Strategy in Action

Listen to the conversations. Is the person expressing sympathy or not?

	Sympathetic	Not Sympathetic
1.		
2.		
3.		
4.		

Discussion Practice

Work with a partner. Take turns finding different ways to express sympathy in the following situations. Then suggest ways of getting over the disappointment.

1. A devoted fan of a long running television program is very upset because the fan club is closing after 20 years.
2. A loyal fan of a baseball team has lost his lucky cap (it was autographed by a very famous baseball player who is no longer alive).
3. A famous singer is getting psychiatric treatment because of the pressure of fans following and harassing her wherever she goes.
4. A group of fans has traveled overseas to see their team play in the final match of a competition. On the way to the game they are delayed and won't make it to the stadium in time.

FURTHER ACTIVITIES

ROLE PLAY

> **Brainstorming:**
> What kind of fan behavior can be harmful? Think of different situations in which obsessive fans can be damaging to the person/team/group they obsess about, to themselves or to their friends and families.

Work with a partner. Act out the following situations.

1. A teenager is trying to convince a friend not to be so obsessive about a pop star or actor.

2. Someone is trying to convince another fan not to be so aggressive when he goes to the games.

3. Someone is trying to persuade his wife/her husband to stop spending so much money and time on buying things related to his/her favorite film star.

4. A parent is trying to get his/her son to get some help because they think he will do something extreme to get the star's attention.

ACTIVITY

Make a list of the advantages and disadvantages of being famous. Work with a partner. Compare your ideas.

Being Famous

Advantages	Disadvantages

SPEECHES - Keep cool

You are the manager of a team that is doing very well this season. It is half-time in an important game. The referee has made some decisions that favor the other team and some of the fans have been getting angry. The organizers have warned that if there are any more incidents, your team will be disqualified. Give a brief speech to the fans.

Consider the following:

• What is the message you want to get across?

• What is the most effective way of talking to this group of people?

• What kind of suggestions can you make for ways of avoiding conflict with your team's fans, the opposing team's fans and the referee?

• How can you keep the speech upbeat while getting your message across?

Give you speech to a group of students. Ask them how effective they think it would be.

CONSOLIDATION AND RECYCLING

BUILDING VOCABULARY

The meaning of what we say can change with different intensifiers. Look at these examples. Then choose the option that completes the statement to reflect how you feel.

1. Hysterical fans at a pop concert can be:
   a. a little irritating.
   b. extremely irritating.
   c. hardly irritating at all.

2. The police should treat stalking:
   a. somewhat seriously.
   b. very seriously.
   c. as seriously as possible.

3. Selling 'official' team souvenirs at very high prices is:
   a. an utter and complete rip off.
   b. a bit of a rip off.
   c. quite a rip off.

4. A person who is an obsessive fan might have:
   a. a slight problem.
   b. a serious problem.
   c. a moderate problem.

5. If I were a celebrity being stalked by a fan, I would:
   a. not be very worried.
   b. be more than a little worried.
   c. be massively worried.

WRITING

Write a fan letter to someone famous you really admire.
Consider the following:
- Why you admire the person.
- What in particular you think is remarkable about the person.
- What kind of influence that person might have had on you.

Read your letter to a group without saying who it's addressed to. Let them guess who it is.

REFLECTION

1. What do you think of fan behavior generally? Is there anything that bothers you about it?
2. Do you ever worry about people becoming too obsessed with celebrity? How important is it to be famous anyway?
3. Is being a devoted fan something that people "grow out of"?

UNIT
12

Strange Weather

Environmentalist and active campaigner, Jen Walsh gives us her opinion on global warming:

The evidence is overwhelming. As far as I am concerned, increased hurricanes in the Atlantic, melting ice at the poles, flooding in Thailand, disappearing islands in Indonesia, and forest fires in the U.S.A. all indicate that global weather patterns are changing. While environmental campaigners, scientists, politicians, and business magnates engage in fierce and often pointless debate about the exact cause, the extent, and the severity of the changes, global weather patterns continue to be affected by our actions and lives are being put at risk.

We might joke about looking forward to warmer summers, but a real threat of drought and desertification looms over some areas of the world while eroding coastlines and rising sea levels menace others. Some models indicate that temperatures could increase by up to 4.5 degrees Celsius by the end of this century. Melting glaciers and the resulting rise in sea levels and temperatures could directly cause changes to wind systems leading to more droughts, floods, fires, and extreme storms. Increased sea temperatures would change the pattern of fish migration and could increase the destruction of coral reefs. Increased air temperatures would result in increased insect populations and the spread of insect-borne diseases. That's not even touching on issues like the effects on water supplies and crop production.

One thing that too many people forget when talking about global warming is the word 'global'. We are all part of this planet and unless we work together to bring in international policies, we will all suffer the consequences together. So what are we doing about it as individuals and collectively?

Some governments are encouraging people to use low energy light bulbs and put solar panels on their roofs, but at the same time they are building new airports and highways and letting industries get away with high levels of pollution. The emphasis is not being placed in the right areas. Or rather, effort needs to be shared by small and big players. Equally, if a small country implements a strong environmental policy, but it happens to be right beside a large country that does not, it seems a little futile. Less developed countries emit less CO_2 than industrialized nations, but are often more vulnerable to the effects of global warming. Unfortunately, with huge political and economic pressure to deny the effects of global warming, the U.S.A. has been reluctant to sign up to some international protocols for carbon reduction. This has given other countries an excuse not to take the radical action needed to really reduce the damage being done. However, more mainstream political figures are now working hard to convince the U.S. government and others that time is running out so perhaps attitudes are changing.

We will all be affected in some way and we can all do small things to use less energy, but what the world really needs is the political will to work together and stop the damage to our planet.

VOCABULARY

Here are some words that will be useful in this unit. How many do you know? Work with a partner to figure out the meaning of any words that you don't know.

carbon emissions	desertification	global warming	policies
carbon footprint	drought	greenhouse effect	rising sea levels
carbon offsetting	erosion of coastlines	melting glaciers	rising temperatures
deforestation	falling crop production	monitor	severe storms

What other words and phrases do you know related to the topic?

VOCABULARY ACTIVITIES

A. List the possible results of the following situations. Work with a partner. Compare your ideas.

Melting glaciers.

No rain and higher temperatures.

The sea or wind hitting the shores.

Too much heat in the north and south poles.

Heat and strong winds over the oceans.

Too much CO_2 in the atmosphere.

Heat being reflected back onto the earth.

Lack of rain over a sustained period of time.

Growing trees to compensate for carbon production.

Lack of water in agricultural areas.

B. Circle the word that best completes each sentence. Then write similar multiple choice questions where the other options are the correct answers. Work with a partner. Answer each other's multiple choice questions.

1. Hurricanes and typhoons are examples of _____ .
    a. severe storms   b. desertification   c. the greenhouse effect

2. When you create CO_2 emissions, you leave a _____ .
    a. rising temperature   b. carbon footprint   c. erosion

3. Farmers in Africa are already starting to see _____ because of drought and desertification.
    a. deforestation   b. rising sea levels   c. falling crop production

4. Scientists have been able to _____ noticeable rises in temperature over the last 20 years.
    a. monitor   b. offset   c. erode

GRAPHIC ORGANIZER

Mark the areas of the world that could be most affected by global warming. Work with a partner. Compare your ideas.

PRE-LISTENING QUESTIONS

1. Do you think about how much energy you use when you travel?
2. Do you worry about the effect you are having on the environment?

SITUATION: *Grace and Abby are discussing what they can do about global warming.*

Grace	I was planning to go to the Maldives this year but now I'll stay closer to home as I'm trying to reduce my carbon footprint.
Abby	Your carbon what?
Grace	You know – the amount of CO_2 I'm responsible for putting into the environment. I'm concerned about global warming and our impact on the environment so I'm trying to do my bit to help. Planes are probably the worst polluters so now I'm only going to places I can get to by less damaging transport like trains instead.
Abby	Look, I'm just as worried as you are but you're not going to save the planet just because you don't go to the Maldives, and you work so hard so why not reward yourself with a nice holiday. After all, I know you do other things like recycling, composting, and not using plastic bags. You already do more than your fair share.
Grace	No, all of that is pointless if I take just one flight. I've also sold my car and take public transport to get to work instead. These things and others like not leaving the TV on standby can help, but the effect is tiny compared to the damage done by flying. I'm concerned that places like the Maldives won't exist at all if we don't all do more.
Abby	You could always offset your carbon emissions by planting some trees when you get back from your vacation if that will make you feel better.
Grace	I'm not so convinced about this carbon offsetting and carbon trading stuff. I think it's a bit of an excuse to just carry on doing what we have been doing for years and not make any fundamental changes.
Abby	Well, I'm with you there. I can't help thinking that if people can just buy carbon credits they will get really complacent. But on the other hand, it's really difficult to tell what can be effective on an individual basis.
Grace	I do think that if everyone does even a little bit, we can all make a difference.
Abby	But the real difference has to be down to governments and big businesses. So, you're really not going to the Maldives?
Grace	That's right. I'm going to go to the coast instead. I can get there by train and there's a resort that I can stay at that's built using sustainable materials.

CHECK FOR UNDERSTANDING

1. Why is Grace not going to the Maldives?
2. What does Abby think about that?
3. Do they both think that carbon trading is a long term solution?
4. How can you reduce your carbon footprint?
5. Do you agree more with Abby or Grace?

Work with a partner. Compare your answers.

Quick Fact
Graduating classes at Thunderbird School of Global Management, U.S.A., are expected to undertake business projects to compensate for the carbon emissions generated during their studies.

PRACTICE AND DISCUSSION

PERSONALIZATION

Complete these sentences with your own ideas.

I am/am not concerned about my carbon footprint because…

I think that global warming is…

I think/don't think that I can…

To stop global warming,…

When people talk about global warming, they usually…

As far as global warming I concerned, I wish that politicians would…

Now share your sentences with a classmate.

DISCUSSION STRATEGIES - Expressing concern

There are a number of ways that we can express concern about something:

I'm worried/concerned about…

I wish that…

I plan to act more carefully when…

It's a shame that…

I can't help thinking that…

It bothers/concerns/worries me that…

I want to think more carefully about…

It makes me uneasy that…

I can't stop thinking about…

Think of more examples.

Discussion Strategy in Action

Listen to the conversations. For each one, write down the way the person expresses concern.

Conversation	Way concern is expressed
1.	_____
2.	_____
3.	_____
4.	_____

Discussion Practice

Work with a partner. Take turns expressing concern about these situations.

1. A reservoir near you that used to have plenty of water is now dried up.

2. Your parents are flying over the Atlantic and you hear there's a terrible hurricane forming.

3. Forest fires have started near where your friends live.

4. The cost of basic food item is increasing becauses of shortages.

FURTHER ACTIVITIES

ROLE PLAY

> **Brainstorming:**
>
> Think of all the things that cause pollution, airplanes, big cars etc.
> How many of these do you have and how many do you really need?
> Think of alternatives to these and arguments in favor of using them.

Work with a partner. For each situation, one student should try to convince the other one to change his/her mind about the decision.

1. 'A' has decided to buy a car. He/She has been saving money for years even though he/she lives in the middle of the city and doesn't really need one. He/she has been using a bicycle for years, but is worried about the danger and the health problems of cycling in a polluted city.

2. 'A' never thinks about where his/her food comes from. He/She thinks it's too much trouble to look at the labels and worry about small things like that. 'B' needs to convince 'A' that things that have been unnecessarily flown around the world can be bad for the environment.

3. 'A' has set aside some money for redecorating his/her house. 'B' needs to convince 'A' that it would be better to spend the money on a more efficient heating system, insulation, and low energy light bulbs.

4. 'A' will only cycle or take public transport, only uses renewable energy, and will only eat local, organic food. 'A' will not go to restaurants or clubs that are not helping protect the environment. As a result, he/she is alienating a lot of friends. 'B' needs to convince 'A' that he/she doesn't need to be so extreme.

ACTIVITY

Make a list of changes in the climate/environment that you have noticed or experienced. Work with a partner and compare your ideas.
Consider the following:

- Differences you have noticed in water levels or water quality.
- Differences you have noticed in air quality.
- Differences you have noticed in temperature throughout the year, when flowers/produce appear, etc.
- Differences you have noticed in weather patterns.
- Differences you have noticed in insect, bird, or animal prevalence and behavior.

SPEECHES - A debate about the environment

Work in groups of up to four people. Each person should choose one of the following points of view and present it to the group for debate.

It's not up to the individual. It's completely in the hands of the politicians and business people.

We don't need to panic, but we should start putting some plans into action.

We are only talking about the problems. We need to act.

We are already in trouble. It is vital that we all start taking action immediately.

Consider the following:

- Examples to back up your argument.
- Convincing language.
- How to clearly and persuasively get your points across.
- How to effectively communicate your level of concern over the issue.

CONSOLIDATION AND RECYCLING

BUILDING VOCABULARY

Write options to complete this survey questionnaire. Work with a partner. Compare your completed questionnaires. Then answer your partner's survey.

1. What is the most important cause of coastline erosion?

    a. _____   b. _____   c. _____

2. What produces the most CO_2?

    a. _____   b. _____   c. _____

3. What are the most serious consequences of global warming?

    a. _____   b. _____   c. _____

4. What do your think are the biggest problems facing Asian countries when it comes to global warming?

    a. _____   b. _____   c. _____

5. What is the most useful thing that you as an individual can do to stop global warming?

    a. _____   b. _____   c. _____

6. What actions can governments and NGOs take to reduce global warming?

    a. _____   b. _____   c. _____

WRITING

Write a brochure for a local community group that is trying to raise awareness of the issues associated with global warming.
Consider the following:

*   The style, layout and presentation that will make the brochure most accessible to certain groups within the community.
*   The most effective approach – gentle, frightening, hard-hitting – for your targeted group.
*   What you want the brochure to lead to e.g.,
    > changing attitudes.
    > raised awareness so they'll ask for more information or attend a meeting.
    > redirection to a website with more information.
    > involvement in a campaign.
*   Think about how you design the brochure so the information can be most clearly communicated.

REFLECTION

1. How can individuals influence a business's policies on environmental issues?
2. Should less developed nations have the same environmental protection policies as developed nations?
3. What will you do to reduce your carbon footprint?

Getting Older

Higher standards of health care and nutrition mean people are living longer. Meanwhile, birth rates in many countries around the world are declining so as a whole, the world's populations are aging. There are widespread concerns over the implications of this. With a larger proportion of a country's population potentially requiring support, how will the younger generations in many countries cope with this burden?

In many countries, we have assumed that older people will always be helped by the governments based on contributions they have made to state pension systems. However, now, even in wealthy countries, many governments haven't planned well enough and they predict a shortfall in pension funds, health care provision, and housing for the elderly. This will mean that although they may not want to think about it, young people need to start saving for their pensions as soon as they start work. This may seem to be a low priority at a time when holidays, meals with friends, buying a home, and starting a family are more important, but it can make the difference between a comfortable retirement and being dependent on others.

Meanwhile, on the African continent, the devastating effects of AIDS mean that a large percentage of the productive adult workforce has been wiped out and rather than being supported by their children, old people are now having to take care of their grandchildren. But what will happen to them when they are no longer capable of taking care of themselves?

Retirement may be a negative concept to those who thought that they were never going to 'get old'. Indeed, they see retirement as the beginning of the end. In many societies, older people no longer live with their families which may increase feelings of isolation and worthlessness. Being unhappy about aging, living in solitude or in an institution, or seeing friends and family die can lead to depression and anxiety. However, to dwell on these aspects means they are blind to the opportunities retirement presents.

Retirement isn't all doom and gloom. Many people look forward to retirement, seeing it as an opportunity to do all kinds of things they could never do while they were working. On leaving their job, retirees may feel they have just been set free. They can travel, learn new skills, get involved in charities or other worthy causes, and just enjoy life.

The people who find retirement exhilarating probably find that they are healthier and happier than at any other time in their lives. They keep doing interesting things, being creative and contributing enormously to society. Others play an important role in the family, being actively involved in the lives of their grandchildren and even great-grandchildren.

The message is clear: old age can be a very positive experience, but you need to make provisions for it while you are young.

VOCABULARY

Here are some words that will be useful in this unit. How many do you know? Work with a partner to figure out the meaning of any words that you don't know.

anxious	pension funds	provision	shortfall
dementia/senility	plan well	require support	side effect
life expectancy	positive outlook	retirees/pensioners	social structures
nursing home	quality of life	retirement	solitude

What other words and phrases do you know related to the topic?

VOCABULARY ACTIVITIES

A. Write the opposites from the list above.

1. be unprepared _____
2. surplus _____
3. be independent _____
4. be relaxed _____

5. childhood _____
6. crowds _____
7. negative attitude _____
8. acute mental powers _____

B. Write the words that best completes the paragraph. Work with a partner. Compare your answers.

How old you are is as much a matter of having a 1. _____ than anything. It also depends on your point of view and the 2. _____ where you live. In some societies, being over 65 and starting 3. _____ means you're old. But if you ask young people, they think that anyone over 40 is old. It also depends a lot on the 4. _____ in your country and the kind of help available when you 5. _____ in life. In Sierra Leone, the average 6. _____ of a man is about 38 years whereas in Norway it's more than twice that.

A lot of people who are 7. _____ about the signs of aging turn to plastic surgery to hide their wrinkles and make themselves feel better. If you have enough money, you can make yourself look much younger. But any surgery can have 8. _____ and should only be taken with caution especially as you get older.

GRAPHIC ORGANIZER

List examples of ways in which your life changes as you get older. Work with a partner. Compare your ideas.

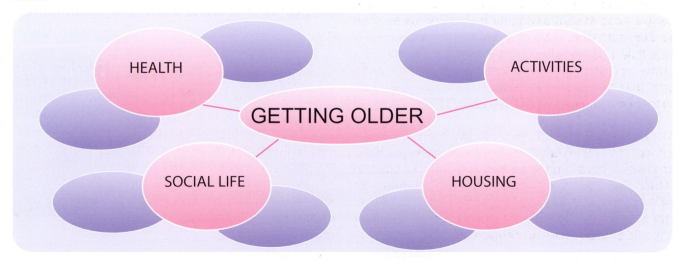

POINTS OF VIEW *Growing old doesn't have to be bad.*

PRE-LISTENING QUESTIONS

1. Do you have elderly relatives who you see regularly? What do you think of their quality of life?
2. What plans are you making for your old age?

SITUATION: *Jacob and Ray are discussing growing old.*

Jacob	I've just started a pension plan.
Ray	Aren't you a little young to be thinking about retirement?
Jacob	Well, the sooner you start, the easier it will be.
Ray	To tell you the truth, I don't really like thinking about getting old. My grandmother is in a nursing home – it's not a very nice place. I never want to get old if it means living like that.
Jacob	I know that getting old can be unpleasant, but it's not all bad.
Ray	What's so good about getting wrinkly and feeble and losing your mind?
Jacob	You could think of it in another way. What about becoming wise and philosophical and not worrying about working and everything?
Ray	Some old people might be wise, but a lot of them become senile and miserable.
Jacob	A positive attitude to aging can make a difference. If you remain busy and especially if you keep your mind active, even if it's just doing a crossword puzzle everyday, you can lead a satisfying life. The trick is to keep your health and to keep busy.
Ray	I see so many people in the home who don't even know where they are. And it smells bad. Honestly, you never want that to happen to you.
Jacob	But it doesn't have to. There are plenty of examples of people who embrace getting old. Look at Jeanne Calment the French woman who took up fencing at 85 and still rode a bicycle at 100. When she was 121, she released a rap record. Now that's aging in style.
Ray	Well maybe some people are blessed with good health into old age, but a lot of people suffer with health problems for many years.
Jacob	I'm not saying that it's easy or pleasant to suffer from poor health, but you can also see it as a journey that you must go through.
Ray	I think that you're overoptimistic. You're trying to cast a positive light on what can be a really unhappy and difficult time.
Jacob	No, what I'm saying is that there's no point burying your head in the sand. Aging is something that we all must face up to at some point. You can't escape it.
Ray	Well, you know the saying, "You're only as old as you feel." I happen to feel extremely young and I plan to keep it that way!

☑ ## CHECK FOR UNDERSTANDING

1. What does Ray see as the problems associated with old age?
2. Why does Jacob think that old age can be a positive period?
3. Why does Jacob mention Jeanne Calment?
4. What do you think the expression "You're only as old as you feel" means?
5. Who do you agree with more, Ray or Jacob?

Work with a partner. Compare your answers.

Quick Fact
Most countries define when an individual is allowed or obliged to do something e.g., voting age, drinking age, age of majority, age of criminal responsibility, marriageable age, and retirement age.

PRACTICE AND DISCUSSION

PERSONALIZATION

Complete these sentences with your own ideas.

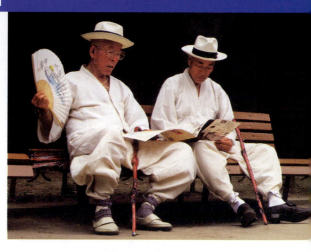

Growing old can be a more positive experience if...

People should treat old people...

I feel sorry for some old people because...

The best/worst thing about growing old is...

One way of improving things for old people is...

Now share your sentences with a classmate.

DISCUSSION STRATEGIES - An alternative point of view

Sometimes it's important to indicate another point of view. Look at these expressions.

...doesn't have to be like that. It can...	**You could think of it in another way...**
What about....	**There are lots of examples of...**
You can also see it as...	**You should consider/think about...**
Did you ever think...	**On the other hand...**

Think of more examples.

Discussion Strategy in Action

Listen to the conversations. For each one, write down how the person gives an alternative point of view.

Conversation   Alternative point of view

1. _____

2. _____

3. _____

4. _____

Discussion Practice

Work with a partner. Take turns introducing an alternative point of view to the following statements. Continue each discussion with further points of view.

1. Old people shouldn't go into nursing homes. They should stay at home with their families.
2. Everyone should be forced to save money for their own retirements because governments won't be able to help them.
3. When you are old, you should take up new hobbies, travel, and keep very busy.
4. Women live longer than men because they're always active with things like cleaning and cooking.
5. More people want to retire in their 50s so that they can enjoy their retirement. However, given that they can expect to live another 20 years or more, they may not have saved enough money.

FURTHER ACTIVITIES

ROLE PLAY

> **Brainstorming:**
> Think of the different problems people face growing up and getting older.

Work with a partner. For each situation, one of you presents your point of view and the other gives an alternative opinion. Keep the discussion going by presenting more opinions. Remember to justify your opinions and support them with facts and examples.

1. A 30-year-old man, married with two children, is considering a new job. It means moving his family 800 km from his aged parents.

2. An old person is traveling and having a good time in retirement, but his/her children are worried that he/she will run out of money soon.

3. A 30-year-old friend is still acting like a teenager. He doesn't see the need to plan for retirement.

4. An old man is becoming senile. The family members are discussing the problems he faces and ways of helping.

5. An old woman is being badly treated in a nursing home, but doesn't know what she can do.

ACTIVITY

With a partner, make a list of the main things that happen in the different stages of life:

- Childhood   _____
- Adolescence   _____
- Young adulthood   _____
- Middle age   _____
- Old age   _____

SPEECHES - What's best for an elderly relative

An elderly relative has serious health problems and cannot take good care of herself at home. Your family is having a meeting about what to do for her. You need to formulate what you think is the best solution and present it to the family.

Consider the following:

- What would make your relative happiest.
- The cost implications of the different alternatives.
- How close they live to the family.
- What sort of resources the family has to offer in terms of physical help, money, accommodation, etc.
- The best way of presenting your point of view to the family.

Work with three partners. Each person should give their talk to the rest of the group (who pretend to be the family). Discuss the various ideas and decide what to do.

CONSOLIDATION AND RECYCLING

BUILDING VOCABULARY

A. Choose the best answer for each sentence. Then work with a partner and compare your answers.

1. I can't stand _____ on others. I'd rather help myself as long as I can.
   a. being independent   **b.** being dependable   **c.** being dependent

2. _____ about a number of minor things can really affect old people.
   a. Anxiety   **b.** Anxious   **c.** Anger

3. We advise young people to start investing in _____ as soon as they start work.
   a. pensioners   **b.** pension funds   **c.** pensionable

4. _____ is on the increase but they are working on new drugs to treat it.
   a. Demented   **b.** Demons   **c.** Dementia

5. If you smoke, your _____ is decreased.
   a. life expectancy   **b.** life expectations   **c.** life experiences

B. Make new sentences with the expressions not used in the activity above.

1. _____

2. _____

3. _____

4. _____

5. _____

WRITING

Write a letter to an elderly relative (real or imagined) you have not seen for a long time.
Consider the following:

- What would interest him/her in terms of your life and activities.
- Things that you might need to explain clearly about anything that you do that they might be unfamiliar with (such as jobs, studies, and technology).
- Ways of expressing interest in their lives and activities and making them feel like an important and valued member of society.
- Be careful not to include things that might offend him/her.

REFLECTION

1. When do you think you will plan your retirement?
2. How/Where do you think you will live when you are old?
3. How do you think you can help old people that you know?

Bullying

Group dynamics and bullying

Although few people feel comfortable talking about it, many of us have been bullied (verbally, psychologically, or physically) at some time in our life. Whether this occurred at school, in the family, in the military, in a sporting context, or at work, the effects can be extremely damaging and long lasting. It is therefore important to study group dynamics to understand why some people bully others and/or become victims of bullying.

Below is a short extract from a questionnaire designed to find out about an individual's social standing.

Please answer all questions. You may check more than one answer.

1. Within a group, there are different roles. Which of these describes your usual position in a group?

   a. a creative and dynamic leader encouraging everyone to participate
   b. passive and somewhat critical
   c. not dominant, but participating actively and offering ideas regularly
   d. manipulating and trying to control the activities of the group

List any other positions you have in a group.

2. Which of these behaviors is a form of bullying?

   a. openly praising and complimenting someone
   b. insulting and belittling someone in front of friends or colleagues because of appearance or actions
   c. secretly helping and supporting someone
   d. constantly finding fault with another person

List other forms of bullying.

3. The following may be a school bully. Give examples of bullying behavior for each.

   a. a teacher
   b. another student
   c. a group of students
   d. a relative

What other people in a school might be bullies?

4. The following may be a workplace bully. Give examples of bullying behavior for each.

   a. someone in a position of power
   b. a colleague
   c. someone in a lower position
   d. an ambitious person

What other people can be bullies at work?

5. Which of the following characteristics do bullies commonly exhibit?

   a. charming and kind in public, but cruel and vicious in private
   b. genuinely caring
   c. wanting to be in control
   d. secretly generous

What are some other common characteristics of bullies?

6. Which are examples of the effects of bullying?

   a. high levels of stress, anxiety, or depression
   b. contentment
   c. low self-confidence and self-esteem
   d. hypersensitivity

What are some other effects bullying can have on victims?

VOCABULARY

Here are some words that will be useful in this unit. How many do you know? Work with a partner to figure out the meaning of any words that you don't know.

belittling	demean	oversensitive	self-belief
confidence	escalate	passive	self-esteem
controlling	finding fault	position of authority/power	support
cruel	low self-confidence	ring leader	undermine

What other words and phrases do you know related to the topic?

VOCABULARY ACTIVITIES

A. Put the words from the list into the correct category. Some words may go into more than one category by changing the word form.

Characteristics of a bully	Characteristics of a victim	Effects of bullying	What victims need

B. Fill in the blanks with a word or phrase from above. Remember to use the correct word form.

What should you do if someone is bullying you?

• Stand up for yourself more and build up your 1. _____. If you need to, take assertiveness training.

• Tell the bully directly how their 2. _____ behavior is affecting you.

• Try using humor or a well-chosen word – the important thing is to say something confidently. This can stop the bullying from 3. _____.

• Check out your body language. If you stoop, hang your head, and hunch over, you may be indicating that you are a victim and signaling your 4. _____. Practice walking with confidence, standing straight with your head held high.

• Tell a person in a 5. _____ what is happening. Give as many details as you can. If you are too nervous to see this person on your own, go with a friend.

GRAPHIC ORGANIZER

Write examples of positive and negative behavior that can occur in the following situations. Work with a partner. Compare your ideas.

AT SCHOOL	Positive:	
	Negative:	
AT WORK	Positive:	
	Negative:	
LOOKING OR ACTING DIFFERENTLY	Positive:	
	Negative:	
DOING OR SAYING SOMETHING UNPOPULAR	Positive:	
	Negative:	

PRE-LISTENING QUESTIONS

1. What is the best way to approach a conflict with others?
2. Do you think that people should ever put up with bad treatment?

SITUATION: *Julie is upset about a situation at work.*

Julie	I'm being bullied at work and I don't know what to do.
Lara	Are you sure you're not just being oversensitive? Perhaps you can talk to your boss?
Julie	She's the one bullying me! At first it was just a few mean comments to me and then she started criticizing me in front of the other employees. Now she makes me look like an idiot when I make the slightest mistake and even blames me for things I haven't done. She's really got it in for me. We're supposed to work as a team, but no one else backs me up in case she starts picking on them as well.
Lara	I know that you can be a bit shy, but isn't there some way of confronting her? Maybe you could work on being a bit more assertive?
Julie	I don't think that would work. To tell the truth, I'm too afraid of her.
Lara	But that's just what bullies feed off. You must let her know that you won't put up with it anymore. Point out that it's bad for everyone's morale and the team's work is suffering because of her attitude.
Julie	That's easy to say when it's not your job on the line.
Lara	Look, you're trying to do a good job for the company and she's stopping you so it's in the company's interest to make her stop. Isn't there someone that you can go to for help? How about her boss?
Julie	Well I could go to the director, but I'm worried I'll be the one that ends up looking bad. She can be incredibly charming when she needs to be.
Lara	You don't have to put up with this abuse. If you can't go to the director, go to the personnel division or get your colleagues to support you. Go to someone else outside the organization. Just don't accept it passively.
Julie	I guess I could talk to my old boss. He always liked me and there were never any problems when I worked for him.

CHECK FOR UNDERSTANDING

1. How is Julie being bullied?
2. Why has Julie not done anything about the situation?
3. What kind of actions does Lara suggest?
4. Do you think that Lara's ideas are useful?
5. Think of other suggestions for resolving the problems.

Work with a partner. Compare your answers.

Quick Fact
One in four workers in the U.K. has experienced bullying at work and half of stress-related illnesses are a direct result of bullying in the workplace. -
www.banbullyingatwork.com

PRACTICE AND DISCUSSION

PERSONALIZATION

Complete these sentences with your own ideas.

You can tell that someone is a bully because…

Some of the reasons children bully other children are…

If you are being badly treated at work or school, you should…

It's important to stand up to others because…

Now share your sentences with a classmate.

DISCUSSION STRATEGIES - Giving constructive criticism

If you have to criticize a person or their behavior, doing so positively can result in a better outcome as you show the person alternatives or options. Here are some ways of giving constructive criticism.

Are you sure you're not…	**I know that you can be a bit … perhaps you could try to…**
Maybe you could…	**You have to … if you want to change anything.**
You need to try and…	**You mustn't be…**
You don't have to be…	**If you … that won't get you very far.**

Think of more examples.

Discussion Strategy in Action

Listen to the conversations. Decide if the person is making a negative criticism or a constructive criticism. Write the words or phrases that indicate this.

Conversation	Criticism	Words or phrases
1.	☐ negative	_____
	☐ constructive	_____
2.	☐ negative	_____
	☐ constructive	_____
3	☐ negative	_____
	☐ constructive	_____
4.	☐ negative	_____
	☐ constructive	_____

Discussion Practice

Work with a partner. Take turns giving constructive criticism in each situation.

1. Your 8-year-old son gives you his painting. He has not been very careful; it was rushed and he didn't keep his brush clean so the colors are rather dark.
2. A student has given a terrible presentation. He was nervous and no one could understand what he was saying as he didn't speak clearly enough.
3. A young woman has wasted the whole day at work because she didn't dare ask what she was supposed to do.
4. A colleague has presented your research to your boss, pretending it was his own work.
5. A teammate has been teasing a new player.

ROLE PLAY

> **Brainstorming:**
>
> Think of the different ways people act and react. How does this affect the way you approach them? What kinds of strategies work best in different situations?

Work with a partner. Choose roles for each situation. Find ways of working constructive criticism into the conversations.

1. A manager (who is a bully) at work is criticizing your colleague's work. The colleague plans to stand up to the boss, but isn't sure what to say.

2. At a party, your friend starts making bad jokes and comments that are offensive about someone else at the party. That person is aware of this and is getting upset.

3. A group of people start treating one of their former friends badly by criticizing her appearance and behavior, ignoring her, and doing things behind her back. One person in the group tries to get the ringleader to stop this behavior.

4. You are visiting your old school and you see the soccer coach picking on one of the boys, humiliating him by criticizing the way he plays, looks, and talks. The boy is very upset.

ACTIVITY

Work with a partner. Describe the best conditions for working with others at college or at work. Consider the following:

- communication styles and techniques
- group dynamics
- working conditions
- roles and responsibilities within the group
- getting the best results

SPEECHES - Reporting an incident

Give an oral report of a bullying incident or conflict within a group (real or imagined). Include the following things:

- Who the report is for.
- Where and when the incident occurred.
- What happened and who was involved.
- What the consequences could be.
- Your recommendation for the best course of action to ensure that it does not happen again. Include what should be done to/for the people involved.

CONSOLIDATION AND RECYCLING

BUILDING VOCABULARY

Add one of the words from the list to the root word in brackets in order to fill in the blanks with the correct expression.

under	over	high	low

1. A person with _____(self-esteem) can find that he/she is a victim of bullying.

2. My sister is _____(sensitive). She gets upset about everything I say.

3. My teacher really _____(reacted) when I got an answer wrong. She was furious and started insulting me.

4. When I decided to take my complaint to a tribunal, I contacted a _____(powered) lawyer to represent me.

5. I knew there was a problem when my colleague started to _____(mine) everything I said in front of all the people who reported to me.

6. It would be a mistake to _____(estimate) the affect that bullying can have on a child or adult.

Work with a partner. Give more examples of behavior for each of the words above.

WRITING

Write an anti-bullying leaflet for a school or work context. Include the following things:

- identify examples of bullying that might take place
- set out a clear anti-bullying policy including actions that will be taken to prevent bullying
- make a list of things to do if/when bullying occurs
- provide details of support that will be provided to bullies and victims of bullying

Consider the following:

- The style of the leaflet and how powerful you want the message to be.
- The type of language you need to use.
- Any symbols, images, or role models you might need to use to help get the message across.
- The people you want to target.
- If you want to include personal examples.

REFLECTION

1. What actions can you take if you are unhappy about a situation at school or at work?
2. Do you think that enough help/support is available to people who have problems with bullying or group conflicts? Should more help be available?
3. How can you help someone who is having a hard time at school or at work?

UNIT 15

Working 9 to 5

It used to be easy. You needed to study a particular course to get a certain job and then you stayed in that job or at least the same industry for the rest of your working life. Now however, the job market is constantly changing. Some jobs such as grocery store cashiers, film developers, and post office workers may not exist in ten year's time while others, particularly those involving new technologies, will develop and expand at great speed.

The problem is trying to read the trends and prepare for them. Just as new technology is likely to replace people in sectors as varied as manufacturing and translation, it will also lead to new jobs in areas like biotech, robotics, and energy industries. Skilled jobs should be safe, but the way in which they are done and their dependence on technology is certain to change. New materials and construction methods have already started to reduce the reliance on skilled trades such as

plumbing, electrical engineering, and carpentry.

Choosing a career involves a lot of research and may involve going back to school. You need to focus on the kind of job which will best suit your strengths and qualifications. It is also about developing the skills, experiences, and attitude that will be necessary in your chosen career. That might include bringing complementary skills such as languages up to scratch. Most jobs will continue to change and you will need to change with them as well as face the possibility of having several different careers.

You also need to think about where and how you want to work. After all, even the most satisfying of jobs is to some extent, just a means to an end – providing money for food, shelter, and clothing. Consider the sacrifices you are willing to make. Would you move to a city where you have no friends or family to get a new job or

commuting several hours a day to get to your workplace? More jobs now allow employees to work from home, sometimes referred to as teleworking, and it is an increasingly popular way of working in many places, but it will not suit everyone.

You also need to consider the working conditions. You may have to work for next to nothing or work long hours in less than satisfactory conditions to gain enough experience to put you on the fast track to promotion. Many young professionals work extremely long hours. Because of the competitive nature of work, many feel that it is necessary to be seen to put in the extra hours in order to succeed. Unfortunately, many of these people burn out after a few years and suffer from depression and health problems brought on by lack of sleep, irregular meals, and high levels of stress. It is very important to get the right balance between work and life.

VOCABULARY

Here are some words that will be useful in this unit. How many do you know? Work with a partner to figure out the meaning of any words that you don't know.

balance	burn out	experience	technology
benefits	career path	perks	teleworking
blue collar	commuting	qualification	updating
biotech	executive	skills	white collar

What other words and phrases do you know related to the topic?

VOCABULARY ACTIVITIES

A. Read the examples and write the words or phrases that they relate to from the list above. Remember to use the correct word form.

1. _____ a degree, a certificate, a diploma
2. _____ able to speak a language, fix things, or use certain equipment
3. _____ feeling exhausted, feeling stressed, feeling depressed
4. _____ director, manager, CEO
5. _____ drugs, DNA fingerprinting, vaccines

B. Choose the words from the list above that best complete the text. Remember to use the correct word form. Work with a partner. Compare your answers.

A lot of people who are fed up with being stuck in traffic while 1. _____ back and forth every day decide to take up 2. _____. In general, people who to do this are 3. _____ workers that have a considerable amount of 4. _____ in the workplace and are well 5. _____. They must have a good relationship with their boss and communicate well over the phone or via the Internet.

Many of those who work from home find that they are able to create a much better work-life 6. _____. However, some worry that they will struggle to maintain strong friendships and will miss the gossip that can be passed on by coworkers. Some people worry about their 7. _____ and future as they might be passed over for higher level 8. _____ jobs if they are not in their office on a regular basis.

GRAPHIC ORGANIZER

Which jobs are going to be more or less in demand in the next ten years? Work with a partner. Compare your ideas.

Jobs in demand

_____
_____
_____
_____
_____

_____
_____
_____
_____
_____

Jobs in decline

PRE-LISTENING QUESTIONS

1. Do/Did you worry about getting a job? How stressful was it?
2. How narrow should your choices be when you decide which jobs to apply for?

SITUATION: *Paige and Jaycee are discussing Jaycee's job prospects.*

Paige	Hi, I didn't hear you come back. How did your job interview go?
Jaycee	Argh, I don't want to talk about it.
Paige	I guess that means it didn't go so well. What happened this time?
Jaycee	I don't know, but I'm so desperate to get a job now that I'll take anything I can get.
Paige	That's not a very good idea. You could waste a lot of time doing something you hate, and if you change your job too often, potential employers will be suspicious. They'll think you're not good at anything or that you can't make a commitment.
Jaycee	But it's much easier getting another job if you're already employed.

Paige	No, it isn't. You don't have time to look around or to go for interviews. It's much better to take your time and make sure a job is right for you.
Jaycee	Do you have to go on about it? Can't we just change the subject?
Paige	Sure. But I think you might be making a mistake by not focusing on what you really want.
Jaycee	Well, maybe that's just the point. I don't know what I want. How does anyone really know until they've had a few jobs? I don't even know what most jobs involve. How can I judge unless I'm open to try anything? Anyway, you can't go for a top job when you're fresh out of university. You have to start at the bottom and work your way up.
Paige	Not necessarily. You've had different holiday jobs and interned at a couple of places so you must have some idea of what you want or at least what you don't want. You just have to do a bit more research, plan a bit better, and decide on a course of action. You've got a good degree so there's no reason to think that you have to start at the bottom.
Jaycee	Well if you're such an expert, how come you have such a lousy job?
Paige	Okay, I think we've talked about this long enough. Let's see what's on TV, shall we?

CHECK FOR UNDERSTANDING

1. What has happened to Jaycee?
2. What is Jaycee's point of view about finding a job?
3. What might potential employers think if Jaycee changes his job too often?
4. How does Paige's point of view differ from Jaycee's?
5. Who do you agree with more, Paige or Jaycee?

Work with a partner. Compare your answers.

Quick Fact
In the U.S.A., women who work full time and have never taken time off to have children earn about 11 percent less than men with equivalent education and experience.

PRACTICE AND DISCUSSION

PERSONALIZATION

Complete these sentences with your own ideas.

When looking for a job, you need to…

To prepare for a new job, you should…

If you haven't got much work experience, you…

Be careful about the jobs you apply for because…

Looking for a new job is difficult because…

The most important things to remember when looking for a job are…

Now share your sentences with a classmate.

DISCUSSION STRATEGIES - Ending a conversation or moving on

Sometimes you don't want to continue talking about a certain topic. You can move the conversation on by introducing a new topic or end the conversation as politely as possible. Here are some expressions that can be used:

Why don't we…
I'm sorry. I don't want to talk about it any more.
We've been over this several times. Can we move on?
I'm not sure there's much more to say about this.
I think that we're never going to agree on this one. Let's…
Can we just agree to disagree?

Let's talk about…
I'm really tired of talking about…
Do you have to keep going on about this?
We've talked about this long enough.
Can we change the subject?
That reminds me. I…

Think of more examples.

Discussion Strategy in Action

Listen to the conversations. In each case, one person tries to change the subject or end the conversation. Was this done politely? Write down the expressions they used.

1. _____

2. _____

3. _____

4. _____

Discussion Practice

Work with a partner. For each of the following situations, one person will try to continue the conversation while the other attempts to end it. Take turns playing each role.

1. You want your partner to give you an introduction to his/her uncle who is in charge of a large fashion company. Your partner doesn't want to do this.

2. Your partner wants to practice her/his pitch for a new contract in front of you, but you are tired and you know that it will be really bad.

3. You want to convince your partner to join you in a direct selling company you are setting up. Your partner doesn't believe it will work.

FURTHER ACTIVITIES

ROLE PLAY

Brainstorming:
Think about the sorts of things that people might ask you during an interview. Think of the kinds of answers you might give to difficult questions such as talking about your strengths and weaknesses. What are some good strategies for an interview situation?

Work with a partner. One of you is interviewing the other for the following jobs. Role play the interview. Take turns as interviewer and interviewee.

Jobs:
- Call center worker
- Teacher
- Executive in a small hotel
- Accountant
- Charity campaigner
- Salesperson
- Health worker
- A job of your choice

ACTIVITY

A. Write a job description for your ideal job. Include the following:

- the job title
- details about what the job required
- location of the job
- rate of pay
- hours of work
- benefits such as holidays, health care, and a company car.

B. You are applying for this job and need to send in your resume. Remember that your resume should present you in the most positive way possible. Don't forget to include the following things:

- your name and contact details including email
- your educational qualifications and skills
- your work experience
- people who will give you personal and professional references

Make sure that it is clearly presented and very concise.

SPEECHES - Present yourself

Make a short introductory presentation about yourself just as you might be required to do in an interview for a new job or a promotion. Consider the following:

- Give some background information about yourself including where you come from and your qualifications.
- Give some information about what makes you unique in a positive way.
- Highlight what's good and interesting. Don't go into any negative aspects of your personality in the speech, but be prepared to answer questions about this afterwards.
- Engage the listener e.g. by maintaining good eye contact and being sincere.
- Keep it short, clear and relevant.
- Be aware of your body language as you give your presentation.

Present yourself to your class or a group of students. You will be asked questions based on your presentation as though you are in a genuine interview.

CONSOLIDATION AND RECYCLING

BUILDING VOCABULARY

Idioms are very common in English. Using them can show a good level of confidence which could be useful in an interview situation. However, if they are used too much or improperly, it can work against you!

There are a lot of idiomatic expressions referring to houses. Match these idioms to their meanings.

1. By the back door.	A.	To get along very well with another person.
2. Drive up the wall.	B.	To talk or do something at length in an unproductive way.
3. Feel at home.	C.	It's free.
4. Get on like a house on fire.	D.	Other people can hear you.
5. Hit the roof.	E.	Something is done in an unofficial or hidden way.
6. It's on the house.	F.	Say or do things that irritate others.
7. Off the wall.	G.	Make yourself relaxed and informal.
8. Take the floor.	H.	It's your turn to speak at a meeting.
9. The writing is on the wall.	I.	To become extremely angry.
10. To go all around the houses.	J.	An unconventional person, idea, etc.
11. _____	K.	A project or endeavor is doomed to fail.

There is an additional meaning. What is the missing idiom?
Work with a partner. Make up short dialogs using each idiom.

WRITING

A good covering letter can be as important as your resume. Write a covering letter to a company to which you are sending your resume.

Include the following:

- A brief introduction of yourself.
- Point out any interesting things about you.
- Elaborate or highlight any points in your resume that you want the employer to focus in on.
- Invite them to respond to you and indicate when you are available for interviews, how to contact you etc.

REFLECTION

1. How do you imagine your career will develop in the next 20 years?
2. Do you think that you will have more than one career in your life?
3. How do you think that you will be able to manage your work/life balance?

Neighbors

QUESTIONNAIRE

How well do you get on with your neighbors?

As we live in closer and closer proximity to other people, most of us will have issues to resolve with neighbors at some point in our life. Complete the questionnaire. Give examples to illustrate each answer.

1 Neighbors can be a real source of help and support particularly if you move from another region or country. However, they can also be a cause of stress if you cannot get along. How would you describe your relations with your closest neighbors?

☐ amicable
☐ polite, but distant
☐ cold
☐ hostile
☐ other _____

2 Sometimes problems with neighbors start small then escalate out of control. Below are some very common neighbor problems. Have you ever experienced any of these?

☐ rudeness
☐ noise
☐ bad smells
☐ animals
☐ other _____

3 Your home is important to you and you need to be comfortable in it. What would you do if you were unhappy about something your neighbor did?

☐ try to ignore it for as long as possible
☐ politely confront the neighbor and try to work it out
☐ ask a third party to intervene or mediate for you
☐ contact the authorities
☐ other _____

4 Sometimes problems with neighbors are not very clear-cut such as making too much noise. At times there can be personality clashes between neighbors. Have you ever been in a situation where:

☐ your neighbor seemed too interested in what you were doing?
☐ your neighbor kept asking you for favors?
☐ your neighbor tried to be too sociable with you even after you made it clear you weren't comfortable with that?
☐ your neighbor had friends and family that you didn't like?
☐ other _____

5 While some neighbors can become like part of your family, other neighbors aren't always the kind of people you would want to spend time with. Sometimes they can even make you nervous. Have you ever been in the situation where:

☐ your neighbors exhibited strange behavior?
☐ your neighbors conducted suspicious activities?
☐ your neighbors threatened you physically or verbally?
☐ your neighbors stole or damaged your property?
☐ other _____

6 Sometimes neighbors can think that you are the problem. Have you ever been in a situation where a neighbor has complained to you about:

- [ ] noise?
- [ ] smells?
- [ ] the appearance of your house/apartment?
- [ ] your behavior or the behavior of your friends/family?
- [ ] other _____

7 Sometimes you neighbor is a business. Have you ever had problems with a business because of:

- [ ] noisy delivery vehicles?
- [ ] being open too late or too early?
- [ ] you didn't like the kind of business it was?
- [ ] their staff or clients were rude and inconsiderate?
- [ ] other _____

8 It's always hard to lose a good friendship but it is particularly bad if you have to see the person every day. Have you ever fallen out with a friendly neighbor? What were the causes?

- [ ] a dispute over property
- [ ] a personal disagreement
- [ ] a dispute over behavior
- [ ] a misunderstanding
- [ ] other _____

9 Sometimes disputes with neighbors can have very bad effects on you and can even lead to health or psychological problems. What are the worst effects of a poor relationship with a neighbor?

- [ ] you can't sleep or concentrate
- [ ] you feel that your environment is dirty or unpleasant
- [ ] you don't feel safe
- [ ] you feel like you're being 'invaded'
- [ ] other _____

10 People have different expectations of what they want from neighbors. Some like a close relationship and others are uncomfortable with that. What is your ideal relationship with a neighbor?

- [ ] to be really good friends
- [ ] to be friendly from a distance
- [ ] to be polite but that's all
- [ ] to have no relationship and remain totally anonymous
- [ ] other _____

BODY IMAGE

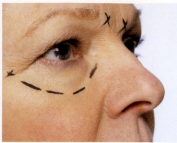

QUESTIONNAIRE

Answer this questionnaire and reflect on how important body image is for you.

1. What do you spend more time/energy on?
   a. your appearance.
   b. learning new skills.
   c. relationships.

2. When you look in the mirror are you
   a. generally happy with what you see?
   b. unhappy with any defects?
   c. unconcerned?

3. When you see someone who looks very good
   a. are you happy because they look nice?
   b. do you compare yourself with him/her and feel inadequate?
   c. try to find fault with how he/she looks?

4. Do you think that in general, your appearance
   a. helps you in life?
   b. gives you a disadvantage in life?
   c. has little to no influence on your life?

5. If you could change anything about your appearance, what would that be?

_____

   Why?

_____

6. List five situations in which plastic surgery can really improve a person's life. Give reasons.

   1. _____

   _____

   2. _____

   _____

   3. _____

   _____

   4. _____

   _____

   5. _____

   _____

PATTERNS & COLLOCATIONS

FEATURED MOVIES

Unit 1 Neighbors (p 06)
The Whole Ten Yards (2004)
Matthew Perry
Director: Howard Deutch
Credit: MHF Zweite Film Academy / The Kobal Collection / Frank Masi

In the Whole Nine Yards, Oz become terrified when Jimmy, a former mob hit man from Chicago, moves next door. Oz is convinced by his wife to go to Chicago to tell the mob where Jimmy now lives. His wife meanwhile hopes Jimmy will kill Oz and she can cash in on life insurance. In this sequel, it is Jimmy's life that is turned upside down when Oz begs him to help rescue his wife from the Hungarian mob led by Jimmy's childhood rival.

Unit 2 Tourism (p 12)
The Beach (1999)
Virginie LeDoyen, Leonardo Di Caprio, Guillaume Canet
Director: Danny Boyle
Credit: 20th Century Fox / The Kobal Collection / Peter Mountain

Richard finds a seemingly unspoiled island paradise where a group of young people has settled. However, the community of drop-outs is driven by the same social evils that Richard was hoping to escape. A group of natives growing drugs in the nearby hills do not appreciate the growing number of foreign visitors. Angry that the new islanders are allowing more people to join their community, they want Richard to be sacrificed in order for the rest to be allowed to remain on the island.

Unit 3 Media Violence (p 18)
15 Minutes (2001)
Edward Burns, Robert De Niro
Director: John Herzfeld
Credit: Industry Ent/New Line / The Kobal Collection / Philip Caruso

Oleg and Emil notice that the media can be used to make a killer appear innocent. They kill well-known Homicide Detective then sell the recording of the murder to a TV show and use the media publicity to avoid a conviction. Emil is paid a million dollars for the tape and becomes a celebrity. Oleg becomes jealous of the attention Emil is receiving and hands over a recording of Emil explaining the plan, thus ensuring both will be found guilty of the terrible crime.

Unit 4 Body Image (p 24)
The Nutty Professor (1996)
Eddie Murphy
Director: Tom Shadyac
Credit: Universal / The Kobal Collection / Bruce MC Broom

Sherman Klump is a brilliant, kind-hearted college professor. He is also very overweight, introverted, and socially inept. He meets Carla, a beautiful and charming woman and falls in love. Sherman's studies lead him to discover a formula that can temporarily change his DNA. He tests the potion on himself and is transformed into a classically good-looking man. He now has the confidence to behave romantically. But is that what Carla really wants?

Unit 5 Cybersafe? (p 30)
Live Free Or Die Hard (2007)
Justin Long, Maggie Q
Director: Len Wiseman
Credit: 20th Century Fox / The Kobal Collection / Frank Masi

Thomas Gabriel gets some of the best computer hackers to work on programs that can be used to destroy the U.S. economy. Detective John McClane brings one of the hackers, Matt Farrell to the FBI for questioning. Not knowing he was working for terrorists, Matt had written an important part of the hacking programs and he knows enough to work out how Thomas Gabriel is shutting down computer systems and what he and Detective McClane must do next.

Unit 6 Modern Families (p 36)
Pursuit Of Happyness (6)
Will Smith, Jaden Smith
Director: Gabriele Muccino
Credit: Columbia / The Kobal Collection / Zade Rosenthal

When Chris loses his family's savings in a poor investment it puts a strain on his marriage. Chris is convinced that he can have more success if he switches career. He has an opportunity to be a stock broker but will first have to go through a grueling six-month internship without pay. His wife leaves. Soon after, he is evicted and he has to take care of his son on his own, sometimes living on the street. He often struggles, but clings to his dream.

Unit 7 Medicine (p 42)
Medicine Man (1992)
Sean Connery, Lorraine Bracco
Director: John McTiernan
Credit: Cinergi / The Kobal Collection

Dr. Campbell, an eccentric scientist working in the Amazon jungle, is close to finding a cure for cancer. However, he cannot replicate the original chemical recipe that successfully treated his test sample. He identifies the missing element, a rare kind of ant, however, his discovery comes too late to stop a logging company's bulldozers from destroying the ant's forest habitat. Campbell moves deeper into the forest in search of the ant and a cure for cancer.

Unit 8 Phobias (p 48)
Snakes On A Plane (2006)
Director: David R. Ellis
Credit: New Line / The Kobal Collection / James Dittiger

Passengers on an airplane include a rapper who suffers from a fear of disease and Tyler, who has a phobia of flying. Their flight gets more terrifying when hundreds of poisonous snakes are released into the cabin in an attempt to kill Sean Jones, a man who had witnessed the brutal murder of an important prosecutor and is traveling to Los Angeles to testify against the murderer. An FBI agent and Sean must now keep the plane in the air and save as many passengers as they can.

Unit 9 Life's Luxuries (p 54)
Marie Antoinette (2006)
Jason Schwartzman, Kirsten Dunst
Director: Sofia Coppola
Credit: Columbia/Pathe/Sony / The Kobal Collection / Leigh Johnson

Despite her privileged lifestyle as queen of France, Marie Antoinette is miserable. She seeks comfort in lavish parties and banquets, spending a fortune on gowns, shoes, jewelry, and gambling. She continues her spending spree, seemingly indifferent to the poverty and growing unrest among the working class. As food shortages grow more frequent riots intensify. The French Revolution comes into full effect in 1795 as an angry mob gathers outside her palace at Versailles.

Unit 10 Good Service (p 60)
Maid in Manhattan (2002)
Bob Hoskins, Jennifer Lopez
Director: Wayne Wang
Credit: *Columbia / The Kobal Collection / Barry Wetcher*

Marisa Ventura is a single mother who works as a maid in a luxury hotel in New York. She is a hard worker, is popular with the other staff and has the potential to be promoted to a managerial level. However, her dreams of a better life for herself and her young son are jeopardized when she is caught trying on some of a guest's expensive designer outfits by Christopher Marshall, the handsome heir to a political dynasty.

Unit 11 Fans (p 66)
The Fan (1996)
Wesley Snipes, Robert De Niro, Andrew J. Ferchland
Director: Tony Scott
Credit: Tri-Star/Mandalay / The Kobal Collection

Gil is excited when his favorite baseball player, Bobby Rayburn, joins his favorite team. Gil is an obsessive fan and neglects both his son and his job to support Bobby even though he is playing the worst season of his career. In fact, Gil will do whatever he thinks is necessary to get Bobby back on form even if that means killing another player. He then kidnaps Bobby's son, telling the baseball star he must hit a home run and dedicate it to Gil, "a true fan," or his son dies.

Unit 12 Strange Weather (p 72)
The Day After Tomorrow (2004)
Paraminder K Nagra
Director: Roland Emmerich
Credit: Tomorrow20th Century Fox / The Kobal Collection

Professor Jack Hall realizes that the rapidly melting polar ice caps is increasing the amount of fresh water in the oceans, diluting the salt level and causing the temperature to quickly drop. A series of extreme weather events is triggered. Tokyo is hit by giant hail, it is snowing in New Delhi, and Los Angeles is destroyed by powerful tornadoes. Within days, the northern hemisphere is subjected to the start of another ice age. While people try to flee south, Jack sets out for New York to save his son.

Unit 13 Getting Older (p 78)
13 Going On 30 (2004)
Jennifer Garner
Director: Gary Winick
Credit: Colombia Tri Star / The Kobal Collection / Sue Melinda Gordon

Instead of allowing 13-year-old Jenna Rink to join their elitist group, some schoolgirls play a humiliating practical joke on her. Jenna hides in a cupboard and wishes that she could just grow up. The next morning her wish appears to have come true as she is now 30 years old and a successful magazine editor. However, she has no friends and no contact with her parents. Perhaps getting older wasn't the best way to improve her life after all.

Unit 14 Bullying (p 84)
Mean Girls (2004)
Amanda Seyfried, Rachel McAdams, Lacey Charbert, Lindsay Lohan
Director: Mark Waters
Credit: Paramount / The Kobal Collection / Michael Gibson

Cady Heron thinks she knows all about the survival of the fittest, however, when she enters public high school for the first time she finds she is ill prepared. Despite quickly making friends with two kind girls, she is drawn into an elite group of the most popular but very mean girls. As Cady spends more time with these girls, she starts acting just like them. Eventually she realizes who her real friends are and apologizes for all the bad things she has said and done.

Unit 15 Working 9 to 5 (p 90)
Boiler Room (2000)
Vin Diesel, Ben Affleck
Director: Ben Younger
Credit: New Line / The Kobal Collection / David Lee

Seth Davis is a college dropout who gets a job as a stock broker and is on the fast track to success. He quickly becomes a terrific salesperson and once his training is over he finds that the pay is astonishing. However, having entered the profession to impress his father, Seth soon realizes he has chosen the wrong company as his job is based on fraudulent business practices, creating artificial demand for stocks. The FBI is interested in him and he needs to get out.

ABOUT THE AUTHORS

Jun Liu

Jun Liu is head of the English department at the University of Arizona as well as Executive Director of the English Language Center, Shantou University, China. His research interests include curriculum development and syllabus design, teacher education, classroom-based second language learning and teaching, and second language reading and writing. He has published in TESOL Quarterly, ELT Journal, Journal of English for Academic Purposes, Journal of Asian Pacific Communication, Asian Journal of English Language Teaching, Language and Intercultural Communication, and Educational Research Quarterly, among others. He is the author of Asian Students' Classroom Communication Patterns in US Universities (Greenwood Publishing Group), and the co-author of Peer Response in Second Language Writing Classrooms (University of Michigan Press). He is co-editor of the Michigan Series on Teaching Multilingual Writers. He is also a columnist for "English Teachers" in the 21st Century Weekly in China.

A recipient of the TESOL Newbury House Award for Excellence in Teaching, and co-founder and Past Chair of Non-Native English Speakers in TESOL Caucus (NNEST), he served on the TESOL Board of Directors serving as Director at Large (2001-2004), and was appointed as TESOL representative in China in 2004. Jun Liu was TESOL President (2006-2007).

Kathryn Harper

Kathryn Harper is a freelance writer, publisher and consultant on educational materials. Her English teaching experience includes teaching refugees, junior secondary students, Canadian Army Cadets, French university students and various groups of business people. She worked for a number of years as an International Publisher for two major publishing companies (Oxford University Press and Macmillan) on their education and ELT lists for Latin America, Europe, Africa and the Middle East. Since becoming freelance, she has done a range of consulting and training, project management as well as writing course books, readers and electronic whiteboard materials. She has written successful ELT courses for countries as diverse as China, Argentina, Cameroon and Spain.